Boy Days

Growing Up in Trinidad

By
Gerry Barrow

Foreword

"Where did he find the time to write a book?" That's the first thing that came to mind when my friend & brother Gerry sent me his manuscript and asked me to write a foreword. My next question was, "Why me?" Nevertheless, undaunted I dove headfirst into the book, trusting that Gerry has always had an uncanny knack for working things out at the end. My 50- year friendship with Gerry is such that either of us could appear outside of the other's home at any hour and say, "Yuh wasting time," and that was a cue to get up and get going on some escapade, no questions asked.

As I read the book, what I found was a fascinating collection of stories of a life well lived; a life with all its foibles, triumphs, a few tears, and many joys. I could not put it down. Gerry is a master storyteller with a sense of humor that colours his perspectives of each encounter and adventure, from a terrifying primary school teacher, a hair-raising escape at sea to a confrontation with a severe storm whilst flying, and everything in-between. Each story leaps out of the pages and has you shaking your head with wonder and amazement that the author "lived to tell the tale". My wife would hear my chuckles and "oh lorse" comments and ask, "You're reading Gerry's book, aren't you?" But, having experienced first-hand what an excursion with Gerry was like, she certainly recognized how it improved her prayer life.

Reading each chapter of the book is like peeling back the layers of Gerry's life. We see the foundation which developed him into a compassionate man who loves the outdoors, has a keen sense of right and wrong based on what people do, not what they say, has amazing talent as an artist, musician, astronomer, photographer, engineering technician, craftsman, and teacher. None of these were his "profession" as a pilot, but all are his passion. What the book reveals are the myriad of threads from his "Boy Days" that wove together to create the character of the 70-year-old man Gerry Barrow. From his childhood in Glencoe dealing with challenges and overcoming obstacles has emerged a man whose talents, skills and accomplishments have positively affected the lives of hundreds of young people.

This book is not only a peek into the way life was lived in Trinidad in a kinder, gentler time but is also an inspirational story for young people struggling to find their place and their "calling" to keep striving and to be true to themselves. It encourages all of us to explore all that life has to offer and to find what excites and enlivens you.

This is a book about a boy from Trinidad in 1960's growing into adulthood and maturity as the country itself attempted to claim its space as an independent nation. Reading Gerry's narrative, one cannot help but wonder how we, as a people, can develop a spirit of adventurism which would enable us to become a self-reliant and confident nation. It was a real pleasure to sit back, read and reminisce about our "Boy Days" and I hope you enjoy it as much as I did.

Dr. Trevor Townsend *B.Sc. Civil Eng (Hons), M.Sc. Civil Eng., Ph.D. Transportation Systems Engineering. R. Eng. (BOETT), C.Eng (UK).*

Reviews

I have long held the view that being a young male is dangerous. Having read this most entertaining narrative; I am convinced that my friend Gerry is not only a gifted "all-rounder" and perpetually young, but has had more than his share of close shaves, many of his own making. The fact that he has survived shows that he is not just lucky but very clever.

A friend of mine once said "when you cease to be a child, you cease to live". I hope Gerry never "grows up".

Dr. David Josa. *MBBS (UWI)and FRCS.*

Having heard almost all these stories from the man himself, it really immortalizes him. Mr. Barrow lived a full life and truly did it all. Unfortunately, times have changed so much that children of this generation will never experience real 'boy days' but this book is as close as it gets to the real thing.

Dr. Andrew Lakan, *MBBS (UWI). Former Astronomy student, Director of the Trinidad and Tobago AstroClub*

Gerry's wife Shaheeba was recently asked, "what is Gerry doing these days?" Her response was, "what is Gerry not doing these days?" This exchange reflects the nature of my fellow QRC boy, the man, and my friend of more than 55 years. Gerry's life as narrated in this book gives a comprehensive and hilarious account of growing up in Trinidad by a multitalented human who experienced the life of ordinary folk through to an accomplished professional. Whatever the reader missed out while growing up can be gained vicariously by reading this book. Take it from me, who Gerry influenced to sell my violin and buy a trumpet to play with him in the QRC Jazz Band so we could meet more girls!

Khalid M. Hassanali, *B.Sc. Mech Eng (UWI), M.Sc. Systems Planning and Optimisation (Lond.), LL.B (Lond.), LPC, ACIArb, Engineer, Attorney- at-law, Mediator/Arbitrator.*

So many LOL moments in this book! The humor brought back memories of V.S. Naipaul's Miguel Street. Gerry has been my friend for over fifty years, and even though I'd heard or experienced several of these stories in real time, somehow, they were even funnier this time around. "Boy Days" took me back to a simpler time. Life as a Trini boy was filled with great fun and cringe- worthy moments for parents.

Neil Chin Aleong, *B. Sc.(Pharm.), MBA, ex QRC head Boy*

Gerry's book is a little more than "Boyhood Days". He gives insights into his family life which are well appreciated. Gerry's father was a pioneer in many fields, serving the community and the nation. With this book Gerry continues the family tradition of service to the community. Gerry's narrative is unique, much in the mold of the man himself telling it as he sees it.

Donald Seecharan, *Bachelor of Laws LLB Attorney at Law and Certified Mediator and Certified Mediation Trainer*

Dedication

This book is dedicated to my parents, Sylvie and Russ, who made me what I am and are equally culpable.

Sylvia and Russell Barrow
1947

Table Of Contents

Introduction

Me with my Mom and sister, Daphne, 1957.

"Get back from there! You know you're top-heavy!" shouted my mother as I peered over the side of the Carenage jetty to see the mullet and garfish swimming in the sea. I was admittedly a little on the pudgy side, but 'top heavy'? WTF did that mean?

To cure this condition she signed me up for ballet lessons with a dance teacher named Helen Mary Kay. The class had about 10 other students, all girls, all white, all pretty. Needless to say, I felt completely out of place, being, fat, brown and ugly. Also, I'd picked my nose and was ordered to go wash my hands.

Ballet is a very demanding discipline, with all the movements and po-sitions given in French. Years later my French teacher would write in my report that I was 'resisting the language'. A lot of time is spent standing on your toes. For a top-heavy guy like me, that was a non-starter. I also hated the sissy ballet shoes. I was glad that none of my friends could see me.

The year ended with a concert at Queens Hall for all the students, including us beginners. We had to do a routine which must have been the 'Dance of the Sugar Plum Bunnies' since we all had to wear rabbit outfits. My Mom bought 2 yards of white toweling material and got the tailor, Chinapoo, to sew my costume. He must have thought a rabbit was a marsupial. While all the girls had small bushy tails, mine stuck out like a kangaroo's. When I did a pirouette the others would jump out of the way.

Since I didn't quite know my part I'd take a cue from the girls. That resulted in a space-time lag between my movements and theirs. This was made more noticeable because of the audible thump I made when I land-ed on the stage.

While I didn't get far with my ballet career I learned to appreciate what's involved in being a prima ballerina. It certainly cured my top heaviness.

Chapter 1

Sylvia in Fyzabad, 2018

My mother Sylvia died recently at the ripe old age of 99. Despite being frail and bedridden, her mind was sharp as a tack and her wonderful sense of humor never failed. She had a difficult life but managed to pull through with grace, which was actually her middle name.

A few years ago my sister and I took her on a road trip to Fyzabad, the town where she was born. It was difficult to find since it's basically a few buildings tucked along a back road. We stopped at the junction where she was able to make out the church and school she attended. Her family moved to Couva when she was ten, but she still remembered everything. This included the names of her teachers and the Presbyterian church ministers.

Walking down the road she saw an old man and asked him if he knew her neighbor, a Mr. Mohansingh. By amazing coincidence, that was the

very guy! He invited us to his home where the two of them spoke excitedly for several hours. True to form my Mom remembered the names of
his twelve brothers, including 'Popo'. That's the nickname she gave the
youngest whom she used to babysit. Ninety years later and the name has
stuck, much to his consternation.

He brought out albums with photos of friends and family, going back
to his grandparents who came to Trinidad as indentured laborers on the
Fatel Rozack. My Mom said her only regret was that she didn't have a picture of her mother. Her parents had separated when she was young and
her ignorant father prevented her and her siblings from seeing her. The
guy said, "Wait a minute," and dug out some more albums. After flicking
through the pages he found a photo of my grandmother. That brought
tears of joy to my Mom's eyes.

Chapter 2

I grew up in Glencoe, a middle-class residential area on the northwest peninsula of Trinidad. It was made up of five streets which branched off from the La Horquette Valley Road. All the streets had Scottish names which were difficult to pronounce. As such, we simply referred to them as First Street, Second Street etc. I lived on Kilbracken Road, i.e. 'First Street'.

When my Dad returned from England as a doctor he took out a $20,000 government loan and bought a house on 10,000sq.ft of lease-hold land. Our spacious yard was used as a football field for all the guys in the area. Behind the house there was a Hi-Lo grocery and a Ross Drugs pharmacy. These would later expand into the busy Highland Plaza.

Glencoe was bordered to the east and south by Newbury Hill and Shorelands respectively. These were rich white communities who kept very much to themselves. One Syrian businessman, on an internationally televised program, foolishly referred to his family as being the top 1%. This moniker has since expanded to encompass all white people living in Trinidad.

There was a hotel in nearby Shorelands with a swimming pool in which you could swim all day for 50 cents. We used to go there often with my mother. One day we met a new receptionist, an old white lady, who told my Mom that the pool was for members only. My Mom accepted it gracefully, but it was my first taste of racial discrimination.

There would be other instances later in life. Once, while my wife and I were strolling through a coastal village in Sicily, a guy came staggering down the hill making monkey noises at us. I thought how pathetic - the village drunk thinking he was better than a pathologist and an airline captain because his skin lacked pigmentation. On another occasion, when fishing on a Cree native reserve in Canada, two drunken young 'braves' drove past in a canoe shouting "Punjabi!" at me. Was that supposed to be an insult? If these idiots could read a map they'd see that Punjab was nowhere near Trinidad. According to the raconteur, Paul Keens-Douglas, "I can't improve your intelligence but I can re- arrange your ignorance."

To the east of Shorelands was the Trinidad Yacht Club. Even though we were not members, we still sneaked past security to bathe. It was there I taught myself to swim by simply letting go of the jetty. It was either swim or sink. I chose the former.

My friend Richard and I once found a leaky old dinghy washed up on the shore. We patched it up and would go rowing far and wide. One weekend we rowed across to Gasparee Island and camped out 'unofficially' in the home of his father's friend, Dennis. The house wasn't locked so I guess he was expecting us. Dennis was a huge, intimidating guy who was a language professor.

Once, at a QRC (Queen's Royal College) 'Old Boys' dinner, the Reverend Clive Abdulah, the Anglican Bishop, gave the opening prayer in Latin. Dennis was the keynote speaker and began by correcting the Bishop's grammar. I, who struggled with Latin, was most impressed.

Rummaging through the house for something to eat, Richard came across his vast collection of Playboy magazines. He went through each one, ripping out the centerfolds for himself. Meanwhile, I found a piece of rubber hose and used it to try and breathe underwater. It didn't work since the water pressure compressed my lungs. I solved the problem by attaching a balloon which forced air down the hose. I was very thrilled to go SCUBA diving. I used my spear gun to shoot a fish which wedged itself between two rocks. I had to pull hard to get it out while it struggled for its life. Even though I eventually succeeded I felt disgusted with myself. I swore never to kill another animal - mosquitoes and cockroaches being the only exceptions.

While fishing off the point, a bunch of young white guys passed us in a new aluminum dinghy. They laughed at our old patched up boat and started 'stoning' us with guavas. When they left I told Richard we needed to arm ourselves since I was sure they would return. We rowed to shore and filled our boat with rocks. As predicted, the white boys soon returned with a fresh supply of ammo. We waited until we saw the blue of their eyes and let loose a barrage of boulders which dented their boat, their heads and their pride.

On the way back home, Richard and his brother Steve got into an argument, and refused to row. Faced with the prospect of drifting to Venezuela, my brother Keith and I donned our fins, jumped into the water and pushed the boat back to Staubles Bay.

Chapter 3

The five streets in Glencoe ended at the river which defined the western boundary. Across the river was the fishing village of Point Cumana, inhabited by underprivileged people. Despite their indigent condition, crime was unknown. The only Indians living there were Mr. Chinapoo, the tailor, and his family. He sewed our school uniforms and did odd jobs. There's a saying about tailor's children having the worst clothes. That was certainly true of his girls. All their dresses were crudely hand-stitched. I guess it was easier to sew new clothes than wash the old ones.

He once came home and asked my Mom if she could pay him again for washing the windows. He said his wife used all the money to buy candles for the church. My Mom, who lived with a Scottish landlady in post-war London, flatly refused. She never spent a bad cent, and was a difficult person to deal with. While every adult in the street was called 'Auntie this' or 'Uncle that', she was known as 'Ma Barrow'. If the cricket ball came into our yard, she would confiscate it. We'd sneak it back when she wasn't looking.

The most colorful character in the junction was Ole' Man Fitz-Allen, a Dutchman who owned most of the land. I'm told that on Friday nights he'd get drunk, ride down the street on his horse and shoot up the place. The next day, when sober, he would pay for the damages. He had his own church which we attended. He gave fiery sermons and handed out 'texts' which we were supposed to memorize (John 3:16 – "For God so loved the world" ... etc.). He had a shed at the back which he leased to Harold La Borde to build his boat, 'Humming Bird', which he used to sail around the world.

His son, Bill, was related to us through marriage since his sister Carmen, was married to my father's uncle Oscar. Bill came into money when his father died and never did a day's work. He was the village ram and the village drunk. He was our favorite uncle since rum made him sweet. He impregnated many of the village women and had a herd of half-naked mulatto children living in his house. We never got to know them even though we figured they were related somehow.

Chapter 4

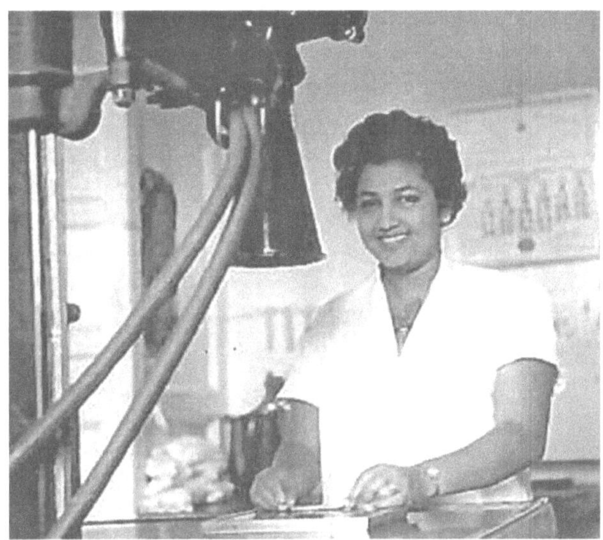

*Sylvia, radiographer at Port of Spain
General Hospital, 1960.*

Growing up in Glencoe was safe and carefree. We were allowed to roam, and most of the time our parents didn't know or care where we were. My mom would cook a pot of mincemeat and macaroni and leave it on the stove. When hungry, we'd take a mouthful from the pot spoon and be off again. We never once sat down at the table to have a meal.

When I was still too young to care, my Dad had gotten involved a beautiful woman named Rita. She was the same 'off-white' color as him. In those days these 'red' women were a rare commodity and, as such, were treated like queens. Indian women referred to them as 'home-wreckers,' and for good reason. They eventually got married and had two kids, Karen and Billy, who are very dear to me. Not having a father in the house was a blessing since there was no one to tell me what to do. I grew up wild, independent and stubborn. It, however, had a profound effect on the life of my elder sister, Daphne.

My Mom was a radiographer at the Port of Spain General hospital. As such she was allowed access to the various Travelling Officer's quarters scattered around the country. Our holidays were spent in remote places like Toco, Matelot and Cedros. Our favorite destination was Mayaro. The caretaker had a 'stringband' of children for us to play with, along with their assortment of goats, dogs and chickens.

With no TV or internet, our nights were spent listening to folk tales about La Diablesse, Douen and Soucouyant. We'd catch crabs in the moonlight and learned to set bird traps and climb coconut trees. We ate delicious 'coconut bread'. That's inside the kernal of a budding coconut plant. Few people know about that.

Chapter 5

My home in Mayaro.

Years later I bought a property in Mayaro to give my kids a taste of that country life. I was lucky to get one of the last remaining beach-front plots in the area. My contractor friend, Ken Harduarsingh, built a beautiful house at minimal cost, employing workmen from the village. He'd purchased a small cement mixer, and while it was running, he put his hand inside to test the consistency. One of the blades cut off his hand and mixed it in with the cement. Doctors were able to re-attach it, but it was never quite the same.

When the roof was finished, I had a 'drink-up' for the villagers. While the women were dancing and having fun some men were off to one side engaged in a serious conversation. As I approached, one of them asked, "Mr. Gerry, you believe a bat could turn into man?" Trying to keep a straight face I said I didn't know - anything is possible in Mayaro.

It seems that one of them came home early to find a man jumping out of his bedroom window. He asked his wife who was it. She said she didn't know.

She was asleep when a bat flew into the room and turned itself into a man. Another guy said the same thing happened to him.

A third one, who also had the experience, said he didn't believe it was a bat. He said he grabbed a cutlass and chased the man across the yard. He said, "Is no way a bat could lick dong a galvanize fence!"

Ken's foreman was a huge guy named 'Killer Whale'. He was the national stick-fighting champion for ten years straight. He looked like he ate cement and bent the half-inch rebar for the ring beam with his bare hands. He was a gentle giant, whose wife would often put him out in the street.

After completing a window, a skinny Indian guy said proudly, "Look! It fit like yam in a nig " That's when he realized it was Whale standing behind him.

Whale said, "Yes, go on."

One weekend my Dad was staying with us, and I asked Whale if he could tell us about stick fighting. Over a flask of puncheon rum he began to expatiate. On Fridays the rum-shop owners would sponsor fights to sell their liquor. People would form a ring and sit on the floor. With drums beating, the two combatants would enter the ring. The referee would inspect their 'bois' for any sharp devices. It seems some fighters would insert a nail at the bottom to gouge out the eyes of their oppo- nents.

I asked him if they used mora wood for the bois. Mora is known as 'iron wood' because of the metallic sound it makes when it falls. It's the hardest wood, and is used for making rafters. He said, "Nah, mora does break. We does use poui. Poui does flex". I couldn't imagine breaking a piece of mora over a man's head.

Everyone in Mayaro had a nickname. I asked my friend Pepe why they called a guy 'Crapo'. Crapaud is the local name for a large toad. He said, "Is because he ent have no neck". Surely enough, the guy's head was resting squarely on his shoulders. The story goes that, when he was small, he and his brother were bathing in the sea. He climbed on his brother's back and dived off, not realizing how shallow the water was. As such, he hit his head on the ground which compressed his neck.

Once, a weird-looking guy came home by me asking for a job. He said his name was 'Chip Chip'. That's what we call the small clam shells that cover the beach in Mayaro. What was strange about him was that his eyes moved in opposite directions. I gave him $20 and asked him to clean up the coconut branches in the yard. He pocketed the money and promptly disappeared.

Sometime later I asked Ken if he knew someone named Chip Chip. He replied, "You mean a guy wid one eye going so and de udder eye going so? Well, actually is because of me dat he eye get so. One night he and another guy came by me in a pick-up selling dry coconut. I said I'd take a hundred and left dem to offload. I came to check on dem and saw Chip Chip putting nuts back in de truck. I hit him one lash in he head with a piece of two by four and he eye fall out. I took him to the Health Centre and dey put de eye back in. I think dey put it in upside down because when one eye go so de udder eye does go so."

My caretaker was a young guy named Vishnu. One weekend I went to Mayaro, and he told me the house had been burgled. Someone broke in and stole my Zeiss binoculars, my onyx chess set which I'd bought in Italy, and my wife's Olympus microscope.

I told Ken and he said, "Is Vish self who tief it".

I said no way. Vishnu had worked for me for several years. I'd even helped him build his house. Ken said he was now on crack cocaine, so that meant nothing. He told me, "Doh worry, I'll get back your ting."

He and Whale found Vishnu in the rum shop. Whale picked him up by the collar and took him to Ken's house. He dropped him on a stool and wrapped a thick ship's rope around his neck. Before he could tighten it, Vishnu told him where he'd hidden the stuff in the 'mang' (mangrove). I wondered who he intended to sell a medical microscope to in the village. Later that afternoon Vishnu came by me to complain about Ken. He said, "Ken Singh did me a violence". I had to laugh. Since then, if anyone ever bothers me I'll threaten to do them a violence. Better still, I'll give my 'pardner' Killer Whale a call.

Another guy who's often on coke, is my present caretaker, Winston, aka 'Squeeny'. When his wife left him, he burned their house down. At the investigation he said he was watching the news when the TV caught fire. The fire department put that as the official cause. I had to help him rebuild his house as well. Once I bought ten gallons of expensive Weather Guard emulsion to repaint my house. Squeeny took the buckets and sold them for$20 each. Soon all the shacks in the area were champagne white. I told him next time he was giving that kind of discount to check me first.

Chapter 6

Richard lived next door and was my best friend. Even though he was black, and I was half Indian, half off-white, our kindergarten friends thought we were brothers. There's no doubt that the best remedy for racial discrimination is innocent kids going to school together. People in our street cared for each other's children like their own, and we frequently slept in their homes. I remember one time when Richard and I foolishly ate some bird peppers we picked from a tree. We started to bawl, and all the neighbors came rushing out, plying us with various home remedies, including brown sugar, condensed milk and Epsom salts.

Kilbracken had its downsides as well, and we were outcasts to some extent. In those days, politicians used race to divide people. It was the 'nigger' People's National Movement, under Dr. Eric William's, against the 'coolie' Democratic Labour Party, under Dr. Rudranath Capildeo. We were the only Indians in the street. I remember once during election time, a loudspeaker car came down the street. The driver shouted, "DLP eh fraid we, buh we eh fraid no damn DLP." Everyone pointed at us and jeered, including Richard, my best friend.

Nothing much has changed, with people still voting along racial lines. Since the number of Africans and Indians in Trinidad is roughly equal, election results are usually close. The two major parties, the PNM and the UNC (United National Congress) exchange power every few years. The only thing that remains the same is 'bobol', the local name for corruption. That's because party financiers who bank-roll the campaigns expect to be repaid many times over. This in the form of bid rigging, over invoicing, nepotism and kickbacks. No one is interested in campaign finance reform so the bobol persists. In Trinidad to be called a 'smart-man' (fraudster) is actually a compliment. It shows initiative.

My paternal grandfather was the manager of Miller Stores on Frederick Street. He would send clothes and toys for us on special occasions. Even though my father was a doctor and we were relatively well off, he never bought anything from the store. Everything was 'second han'. In those days there was no such thing as planned obsolescence. Things were built to last, and anything that broke was repaired.

Old knives and scissors were sharpened by a man with a grindstone on his bicycle. Salesmen would come door to door with a large selection of brooms and brushes. Syrians sold fabric from suitcases. They would later open large department stores with questionable financing. The only people still walking the streets are the Jehovah Witness with their Watchtower magazines. I'd buy a copy but spare me the sermon please.

Our Saturday mornings were spent at A.M. Querino auction sales, where all our furniture and appliances were purchased. These sales were a great source of entertainment, with the auctioneer taking bids at lightning speed. My dad once bought a rusty old toaster, which was quite a novelty. Unfortunately the hot toast soaked up a lot of butter, which impacted negatively on his grocery bill. He threatened to get rid of the toaster, so I learned to scrape the butter quickly over the toast before it could soak in.

Chapter 7

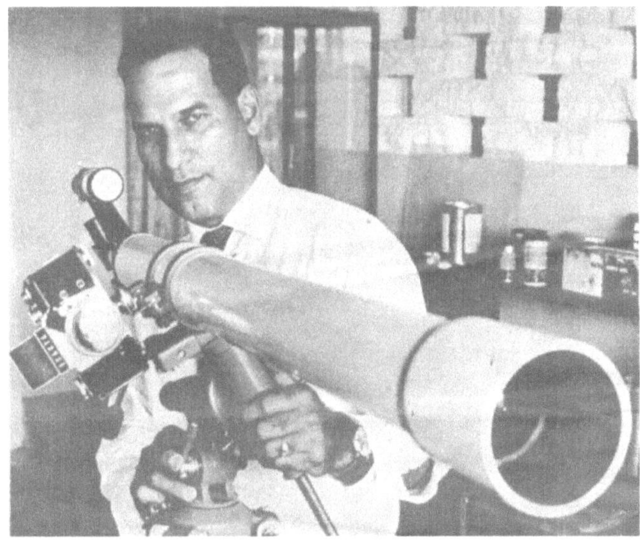

Russ, 1964

My father, Dr. Russell Barrow, was the most brilliant man I ever knew. He was an over-achiever in many fields, including photography, amateur radio, computers, horticulture, ornithology, theology, meteorology, electronics and astronomy, just to name a few. And those were just his hobbies.

In 1944 he entered McGill University, Montreal, to study electrical engineering, and served with the Royal Canadian Air Force. Knowing the financial strain on his father, he accepted a British Government scholarship to study medicine at King's College Medical School in London. There he played hockey, built a working model steam locomotive and a TV with an upside down picture.

He joined the local chapter of his fundamentalist church, the Gospel Hall. The minister introduced him to the congregation as a brother and asked him to say a prayer in Latin. Not knowing the first word, my father solemnly recited the name of the muscle that moves the nostril. It's the smallest muscle in the body but has the longest latin name. Everyone said "Amen"

He returned to Trinidad in 1952 and worked as an anaesthetist at San Fernando. Until his retirement in 1980 he served as senior radiologist in the country. From 1974-76 he was also acting Medical Director of the Port of Spain General Hospital. In 1986 he was awarded the Scroll of Honour by the Trinidad and Tobago Medical Association for outstanding service to the cause of medicine. In 1990 he was elected a member of the Caribbean Academy of Sciences. The country finally honoured him in 1993 by awarding him the Chaconia Medal (Gold).

Listing his accomplishments would fill a library. He would get into something, reach professional level, then drop it completely, and do something else. He discovered two new species of orchids which he graciously named after someone else. Even though he wasn't a professional photographer, his door was covered with 'First Place' ribbons from the professional photographer's competitions.

He was a knowledgeable bird watcher and published a bird atlas based on his photos. He had his pilot's license and used to take me flying. This nurtured my dream of becoming a pilot. Even though he was tone-deaf he bought me my first guitar. Meanwhile my Mom used her limited resources sources to get me me a piano and trumpet. My love of music continues to this day.

'Russ' was known as 9Y4-RB (Rubber Band) to the 'ham' (Amateur) radio community. I would sit in his 'shack' and listen while he established CQ (seek you) contacts from around the world. One such call came from a US serviceman stationed in a tent near the north pole. After a while his signal began to fade. He looked outside and saw a polar bear interfering with his antenna. He said to hang while he went out to chase it away. After a few anxious moments we were relieved when he eventually came back on air. I would later to go on to get my radio license, call sign as 9Y4-GB (Grand Boca)

Unfortunately my Dad is probably best known for his involvement in the Dalip Singh murder case. Dalip and my Dad knew each other in England as medical students. He was engaged to a German woman name Inge. As Jewish children, she and her sister were smuggled out of Nazi Germany and cared for by a Scottish family. My mother would often use her ration coupons to provide dinner for them. When, as qualified doctors, they returned to Trinidad and had little contact with each other.

Dalip and Inge got married, but things didn't work out. One day in1954, he asked my Dad to borrow his textbook on anatomy and his surgical instruments. He murdered his wife and used my dad's tools to cut up her body, which he put in a sack and dumped in the sea. It washed up on the beach sometime later.

That day Dalip dropped by my Mom, which was strange since they had not seen each other for quite a while. She called my Dad, who told her he was doing a postmortem on a white woman. On hearing this Dalip said he'd go and assist. Little did my Dad know that the woman on the slab was Inge. Dalip pretended he didn't know either.

It took a while, but Singh was eventually arrested and charged with murder. During the trial my Dad testified that, whoever cut up Inge's body, had a knowledge of anatomy. He'd done a neat job. Singh was found guilty, and remains the only doctor in Trinidad to be hanged.

Chapter 8

My dad teaching how to 'star-hop' at the Trinidad and Tobago Astronomical society, 1965.

On a less gory note, my Dad is also remembered for founding the Trinidad and Tobago Astronomical Society. He was its president for the first 10 years. During that time he photographed comets, timed occultation's and gave slide show presentations of his deep-sky photographs.

Early one morning he woke up my brother Keith and me to see comet Ikeya-Seki streaking across the eastern sky. It was a fantastic sight, and I was hooked. I was about 10 years old and started attending the meetings.

Despite my Dad's renown, he was humble and down to earth. He was an avid hunter and fisherman. Once, as a teenager, I'd gotten a summer job in the biochemistry lab at Port of Spain General Hospital. The Minister of Healthwas touring the facility. Mr. Young, our biochemist, was introducing him to the lab techs. When he got to me, he said "This is Gerry Barrow, Russell Barrow's son."

"Who?" Asked the minister.

I expected him to say, "Russell Barrow, the consultant radiologist at the hospital".

Instead he said "Don't you know Russell Barrow? The fisherman?" Turns out that my Dad and Mr. Young were old fishing buddies.

Chapter 9

Iere High School visit, 2018

Fifty years later I founded the Trinidad and Tobago AstroClub (TTAC), a vibrant student-based astronomy organization. Its purpose is to encourage the formation of astronomy clubs in schools. As such, when invited, we'd visit schools and give presentations, demonstrations and viewing sessions all over the country.

TTAC AstroQuiz Competition

We have many exciting activities including our national AstroQuiz competition in which 18 of the top schools in the country compete for a telescope prize. At our summer camp at my property in Mayaro we divide 60 students into 4 'tribes' who compete against each other at everything, including cooking, watersports and talent.

TTAC Band – The Lunartix.

29

Chapter 10

TTAC Executive 2023-

The Astro Club is now managed by Candice, a director and founding member. She is ably assisted by dedicated 'seniors', ex-students who have remained to manage things. TTAC is my pride and joy, and a fitting tribute to my father.

Model of the Saturn V Apollo Moon Rocket

Since we don't charge students for anything we raise funds by having a 'Star Party' open to the public. We try to have some exciting activities, such as the 'launch' of a 16 ft Saturn V rocket a few years ago.

During a radio interview to promote this event the host asked Andrew, our most senior member, "Who built the rocket?" He replied "Mr. Barrow. He can do anything." Well, not quite. Andrew is on his way to becoming a specialist physician while I was too duncy to get into Med School.

Chapter 11

Andrew with our 16"telescope mirror

I first heard of Andrew while doing one of my coaching sessions at Holy Cross College. One of the students told me that Andrew considered me like a father. I asked, "Which one is Andrew?" I would soon find out.

Even at the age of 14 he was exceptionally bright and capable. With a less than ideal home situation he supported himself through A-levels by working as a linesman with T&TEC, the electricity company. He'd have to do disconnections in the roughest areas where others were afraid to go. With his keen interest in astronomy and computer savvy he became the astrophotography instructor at our observatory.

We shared an interest in many other things, including fishing and trail bike riding. One day we decided to try and get to Maracas Bay by riding over El Tucuche, which at 3,100 ft, is the second highest mountain in Trinidad.

The trail was narrow and muddy, with a cliff on one side and a precipice on the other. We came to a spot where a rock fall obstructed our path. Not sure if to proceed, we saw a guy sitting nearby and asked him if the trail got any better. He said it got worse but there was a rope on the side of the hill you could hold onto. He said he rode there once and slid down the precipice. He was on a fishing trip so was able to weave his nylon lines into a rope and haul himself up. Andrew and I looked at each other, thought about it and said, "F dat!"

My previous bike was a Suzuki SV 1000 sports model. I used to go to work on it, and the trip from Valsayn to Piarco would take 7 minutes flat. One morning I left home at 4:00am and there was a slight drizzle. I should have turned back and used the car. I continued however, thinking, "How wet can I get?" By the time I got on the highway the rain was falling heavily. At the airport I had to wring my socks and pour water out of my shoes. For the rest of the day I flew the plane barefooted with my wet shirt open.

On another occasion a guy broke a major road and crossed in front of me. To avoid a collision I jammed the brakes and threw the bike over to one side. It landed on my leg, trapping me below. Worse yet, gasoline started to leak over me. The bike was very heavy, and my shoes had melted. I couldn't get a grip to lift it off. I was also concerned about the hot muffler igniting the gas fumes. If so, I'd be toast. Eventually someone stopped and helped me up. I realized that bike was going to kill me sooner or later. The temptation to go at breakneck speed was too great.

I traded it in for a Yamaha XT 250 trail bike which was lighter and could handle the bad country roads I liked to explore. The first day I got it I went riding through the central range. I came to a fork in the road and asked an old man sitting there for directions. He said to the right was Mamural, and the left was Tamana, but that road was bad. Of course I went left. What started as a road soon turned into a track, which then disappeared entirely. I was riding through dense forest for miles, through mud, over logs and across ravines.

Stopping to get my bearings I saw that there were no bars on my phone. It dawned on me that, if my untested bike broke down, I had no way to contact my son Khalid, a search and rescue helicopter pilot. Even if I could reach him, I had no idea where I was. I pressed on through the bush and eventually emerged at Tamana #3, way out to the east.

Afterwards my wife insisted that I ride with someone from then on. To keep her from worrying I invented a riding partner named Mike, who I would meet along the way. She once asked how come I never invited him home. I told her he's kinda shy and introverted.

Chapter 12

*Using our new 16"computerized telescope at
the TTAC Observatory*

On Friday nights, during the dry season, we do astrophotography at my home observatory. This is a complex highly computerized process in which it takes many hours to get one image. If done correctly you'd think the photo came from the Hubble.

*M 42, The Orion Nebula,
taken by my students at the
TTC observatory*

Chapter 13

Andrew and Penny at the launch

Ten years after my retirement, at age 68, I decided to get into sailing. Shaheeba and I enrolled in a sailing course and did better than the youngsters, who kept capsizing or falling out their boats. Afterwards I purchased a 50- year-old Tartan 34ft yacht which had been lying derelict for many years. It took me 6 months to get it back in ship-shape condition.

Andrew and his fiancée Penny installed all the electric equipment, which included solar panels, navigation lights, lithium batteries, a generator and inverter. I handled the rigging and woodwork, while my handyman Sheldon did the plumbing and painting. Along with Shaheeba, they make up my sailing crew. At its launch an elderly 'yachtie' couple remarked, "What a pretty boat", and they had a floating palace!

Sailing is a relaxing pastime but has its ups and downs. On one occasion, before a race, we were using our small wooden dinghy to get to the yacht. It was a bit overloaded, with five adults on a boat designed for four. While standing on the gunnel to climb onto the yacht, water started coming in over the side. In no time the dinghy flooded and started to sink. Andrew, who was standing on the dive platform, tried to hold onto it with the chain. I was thrown into the water, along with Marcus, one of our crew.

The current was very strong and was sweeping us away. I had the heavy toolbox in my hand which was pulling me down. I started to get annoyed since I felt it was trying to drown me. It was difficult trying to swim with one hand while having to come up occasionally for a breath. I reluctantly had to let go of the toolbox which had my keys.

With the help of our boating neighbor, Kilby, who came with his dinghy, we managed to refloat ours. By this time Andrew's arms were sore but we were able to make it to the race on time. I took the plunge afterwards and bought an inflatable dinghy which is far more stable. You live and you learn.

While you can get a second hand yacht for less than the price of a used car, the maintenance cost is prohibitive. Anything associated with boats is expensive. For every hour you spend sailing you spend a week fixing. The sea is a very hostile environment and everything corrodes after a while. Fortunately my crew is highly skilled, so my labour cost is minimum. Working on the old boat is something we enjoy.

Chapter 14

My Dad's hunting partner was his 'pumpkin-vine' cousin, Sonny Boy. They used to hunt in Chaguaramas, a restricted US naval base at the time. When my Dad expressed concern about this Sonny replied, "Doh worry – de captain an me is good buddy."

Sonny was a colorful character and would often boast how he'd 'nailed a gouti' or 'jammed a carite'. You had to be careful when fishing with him. Fishermen are very superstitious folk, and any little thing could cause 'pelasse', in which you caught nothing all day.

One day, while hunting, they shot an agouti. My Dad realized it was pregnant and did a Caesarian section. He delivered two babies and brought one back for Keith and me. It was our pet for a long time. It used to follow us through the bush – something the hunters found hard to believe.

Such 'wild meat' as agouti, lapp, quenk, tattoo and manicou are local delicacies, but I remain passionately opposed to all forms of hunting. It's as if the poor creatures don't have enough problems without being chased by dogs, smoked out of logs or blinded by lights while drinking from a pond. My words to hunters are, "If you're hungry go buy some KFC and leave our endangered animals alone."

As for fishing, my Dad would wake up Keith and me at 4:00am on Saturday mornings. We'd go out on the north coast and spend all day banking in the rough open sea. The fact that I never get seasick probably has something to do with that early training.

One day a huge manta ray passed under the boat. I could see the tips of its wings on either side of the boat, like two sharks cruising. The anchor rope got caught in its horns and it started dragging us towards Venezuela. My dad had no choice but to cut the rope, losing his anchor in the process. This was a common and expensive occurrence. As such, mantas were called 'Devil Fish' by the local fishermen, even though they were otherwise harmless.

Another common creature in our waters are turtles. Our eastern beaches are popular nesting sites for giant leatherbacks. Fortunately, efforts are finally being made to protect them, since once they start laying their eggs, they are defenseless.

While fishing, my dad once grabbed his gaff and pulled a large green turtle into the boat. I guess he had plans to make soup later, but Keith and I insisted he release it. We drove to a nearby beach and played with it for a while before it went on its way.

One memorable day my Dad and I stayed out late and caught thirty-five huge redfish. The water was 200ft. deep and we were pulling them up two at a time. On the way back I drove the boat while he cleaned the fish. I was about eleven at the time but was an experienced driver.

While rinsing a fish it slipped out of his hand. He dived off the moving boat and disappeared into the darkness. Alarmed, I turned the boat around to look for him but couldn't see a thing. Eventually, he surfaced some distance away with the fish in his hand. I told him he was mad — we had thirty-four other fish in the boat! He said, "Yes, but this was the biggest one." When we got home, he cleared out the freezer and we ate redfish for the next 3 months.

Sometime after, I went snorkeling with him in the first boca. As we got further out to sea I started to feel uneasy. I have this unnatural fear of sharks sneaking up on me. In our murky waters I wouldn't see them. I motioned that we should head back, but he kept on going. By now I was too scared to continue and too scared to go back on my own.

That's when I saw the coils of a large spotted moray eel protruding from beneath a rock. I pointed it out to him, indicating let's get the hell out of here! Instead, he took his stick and poked the eel, which darted off in a flash. By now I was convinced that my father was not just mad, he was a raving bi-polar schizophrenic. I raced back to the shore at high speed, barely touching the water along the way.

Our boat was an old wooden pirogue which used to leak. Pirogues had a unique design whereby the hull was built by wrapping boards of white pine around a central 'shell' and working your way up. This gave them a deep narrow shape, ideal for our rough waters. Once the hull was complete, ribs made of hard crapaud wood would be shaped and fitted to add strength. This was a departure from usual boat construction, where the ribs are made first. Fiber 'wick' was shoved between the boards and sealed with putty to make them watertight. This never worked very well and all pirogues leaked. Every fishing boat had a calabash or Klim tin to use as a bailer.

Around that time fiberglass was becoming popular, so Keith and I decided to cover the hull with that expensive material. To do so we'd have to drive the boat from its mooring in Staubles Bay to a slipway in Pt. Cumana. From then we'd get some fishermen to help drag it to our house, rolling it on logs.

In those days you didn't pay people for help, we all pulled together. They just needed a nip of puncheon rum to 'wet their teeth'. They would then throw some on the ground for good luck. All fishermen communicated in patois, a kind of broken French still spoken in St. Lucia. It kept the white bosses from knowing what they were saying about them.

That day there was a big storm, with heavy rain and thunder. Keith and I set off anyway. With us there was no such thing as fear, only tunnel vision and rank stupidity. While passing Point Gourde an enormous wave lifted the boat which came down with a sickening crunch. It loosened some of the calking between the boards and water came gushing in like a fountain. I threw my shirt for Keith to plug the hole. By the time he stopped the leak, the water was up to the gunnel.

We rounded the point and managed to get to Carenage before it sank. There I saw a Shouter Baptist priest baptizing some women in the sea. I asked him to borrow his calabash and used it to bail the boat. It took a long time, while the devotees stood and waited impatiently for their salvation.

There is a story about a priest baptizing a woman in Mayaro, when a big wave broke and washed her away.

The priest turned to the others on the beach and said, "De lord giveth an de lord taketh away. Sen ah nex one!"

Chapter 15

Suzie on my pirogue, Zangee

Later in life, I bought a 28 ft. fiberglass pirogue, built by Brian Bowen. He was a brilliant young designer whose powerboats like 'Mr. Solo' and 'Checkmate' usually won the Great Race to Tobago. He was married to Janelle 'Penny' Commissiong - Miss Universe 1977. Unfortunately he was tragically killed while cycling one evening in Chaguaramas. A company continues to make beautiful boats using his molds.

I named my boat named 'Zangee' after a fresh water eel. These are feared by men who go in the swamps to catch crabs. It's said they have a large tooth and can bite your toe. I planned to keep the boat at my beach house in Mayaro, and sank a concrete mooring just beyond the breakers. When I got the call that it was ready I drove to Chaguaramas, jumped in the boat, along with Shaheeba and my son Mickhaiel.

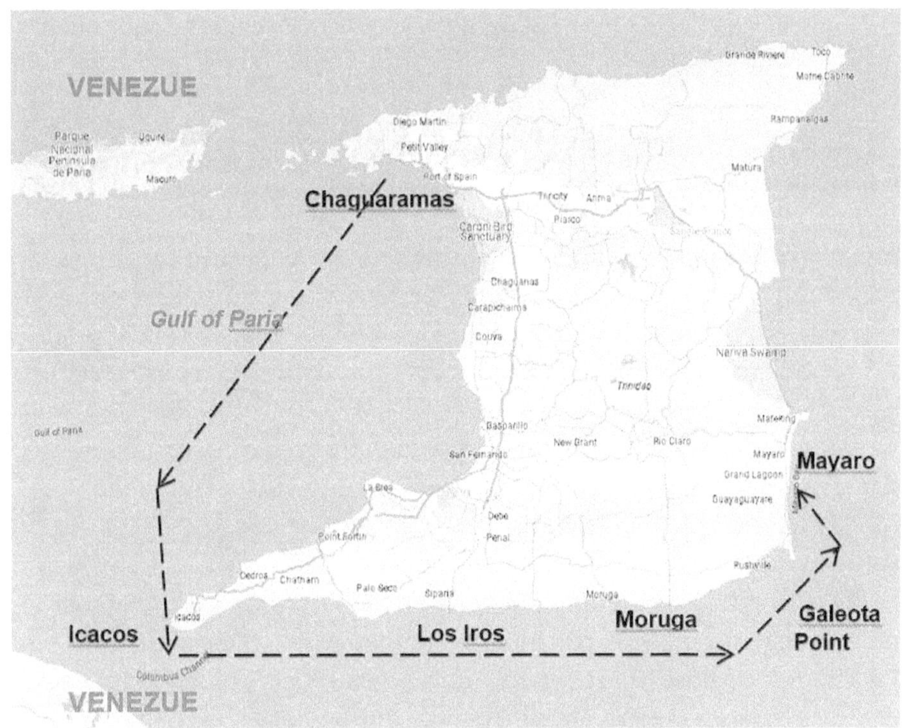

The trip from Chagaramus to Mayaro.

The route I planned would take us from Chaguaramas to Icacos, the southwestern tip of Trinidad. We'd then drive along the south coast to Galeota, the southeastern point. From there we'd head north to Mayaro. I estimated the trip would take about 6 hours but the water in the Gulf of Paria was unusually rough. Within minutes Micky was lying down on the back seat sea sick.

Without proper nautical charts, I'd used a primary school atlas with a map of Trinidad to navigate towards Icacos. When I reached my ETA (Estimated Time of Arrival) there was no land in sight. I checked my GPS coordinates and realized we were in Venezuelan territorial waters. Expecting the dreaded 'Guardia' to appear at any moment I made a quick course correction.

We arrived at Icacos at dusk and were greeted with a magical sight. There were dozens of abandoned oil platforms in the sea, with people living on them. As far as you could see came the warm glow of kerosene lamps. It was like a scene from the movie Water World. I doubt many people know about this.

The next leg of our journey took us along the south coast. By then it was pitch dark. As we passed the coastal villages of Moruga and Los Iros people flashed lights at us. These were smugglers thinking we were bringing in their consignment of guns and drugs. I speeded up in case they thought we were skimming and started shooting at us. This porous coastline is very near to Venezuela and is a popular transshipment point for contraband. Every month dozens of Venezuelans migrants arrive here to escape the economic hardships in their country. While some people complain, I say the more the merrier. All the Venezuelans I know are decent hardworking people. Slack Trini workers, living on their phones, can learn a thing or two from them.

We reached Galeota Point around 9:00 pm. We had been out of cellphone range for most of the trip. My mother was convinced that we were lost. She alerted the Coast Guard who said they'd go look for us the next day. By now we were in sight of Mayaro. The miles of deserted beach were black except for a fire which Khalid had thoughtfully lit for us. He is now a helicopter captain and knows the area well since his company, Bristow, services the BP oil rigs off the east coast.

I dropped Shaheeba and Micky on the beach. I then drove the boat out beyond the breakers, tied it to the buoy and swam back to shore. The next morning the local fishermen came out to see how I was going to get it into the boat house I'd built. I put the trailer in the water using a small tractor I'd purchased for the purpose. I then swam back to the boat and drove it onto the trailer. That's as far as I got.

Under the enormous weight, the wheels of the trailer sank deep into the sand. I'd anticipated this but expected the tractor to pull it out. No such luck, it wouldn't budge. Eventually, my contractor friend Ken brought his back-hoe but even that wasn't working. By now a large crowd had gathered, excited to see what would happen next. Ken revved the engine and the front of the tractor lifted high into the air. It came down with a crash which pulled the trailer free. He got a loud round of applause from the gathered community. That was their excitement for the day.

I realized that keeping the boat in Mayaro was not practical. My Dad had told me as much but, being 'harden', I thought I knew better. We now keep it safe at Power Boats in Chaguaramas. After 25 years it still looks brand new.

Mayaro fishing boat

Chapter 16

A year later we made a trip to the Grenadines on Zangee. These are a group of islands south of St. Vincent, and is a popular destination for 'yachties' from around the world. I spent a week there with my family. Each day we'd visit one of the islands, including the Tobago Keys, surely one of the most beautiful places on Earth.

When it was time to return, a tropical storm was closing in. I wish I could have remained on Union Island and waited it out, but I had to work the next day. I left early, with my two young sons and a fisherman friend named Glen. We carried duplicate safety equipment, including flares, radios and a life raft. I tried to outrun the storm, with my two 100 HP Mercury engines pushing us at 30 knots. No such luck, the storm caught us at Kick'em Jenny.

Kick'em Jenny is an underwater volcano located between the islands of Carriacou and Grenada. It is one of the most active submarine volcanoes in the Eastern Caribbean. According to legend, Jenny was an unfaithful woman who met a tragic fate. Her spirit was said to be restless, causing the turbulent water in the area. Under normal circumstances it is the roughest part of the Caribbean. Add a tropical storm and it gets real nasty.

I'd never seen such big waves in my life. They'd pick us up and we'd go skating down the side. I struggled to maintain directional control to avoid rolling over. Apart from the main swells, there was severe chop hitting us from all directions. It was like being in a giant washing machine on steroids. Lightning was flashing all around and I could barely see because the raindrops were hitting my eyeballs like buckshot.

The ordeal lasted for an hour while my sons, huddled under a tarpaulin, were laughing and enjoying the adventure. With zero visibility I depended entirely on my GPS to guide us home. This included passing blindly past the 'tooth,' a vertical rock located in the narrow 'first boca' passage along the way. The weather broke just as we arrived in Chaguaramas several hours later, safe and sound. I silently thanked Brian for building such an amazing boat.

Last year Shaheeba and I did a sailing course and went racing with friends to gain experience. We plan to make another trip to the Grenadines in Easter. This time we'll be sailing in my 50-year-old yacht which I named it Sofiya, after my precious daughter Sofi.

Chapter 17

Sailing my model boat, 1964

There were many characters living on our street. I'll describe some of them for you, plus a few interesting events to the best of my recollection.

At the top of the road lived the Bains. Their son Ashley was older than me and completely reckless. He once gave me a 'tow' on his bike which could have ended badly. We started at the top of Newbury Hill above La Horquette Road and came rushing down at great speed. It was quite exhilarating since he had no brakes. Ashley's theory was that, if you crossed the main road fast enough, you could avoid being hit by a passing car. It made sense at the time.

Next door lived Richard's parents, Joan and Kester Mailin-Smith, a bi-racial couple. Kester was a manager at H. E. Robinson, agent for Hillman cars. My brother-in-law, Ian Carvalho, worked for him. He used to drop Richard at home, which is how he met my sister Daphne. They eventually got married and have a daughter, Kellie. Even though Joan had only one lung she was very active. Richard and I used to go with them in the forest to collect plants and pick guavas for making jam. We'd have guava fights on the way back.

We were both into model boats. We'd build yachts and sail them at Tembladora Bay on weekends. We also used to steal comic books in Hi-Lo by hiding them under our jerseys. A guy named 'Poonky' from Pt. Cumana, who limed with us, decided to try his luck. Instead of hiding a comic book, he put a frozen chicken under his shirt and was caught. His excuse was, "Ah was hungry like forty rat who ent eat for forty days."

I still build model planes, rockets and radio-controlled boats, such as 'Nemesis, a FPB (Fast Patrol Boat) which I 'scratch built' out of fiberglass and teak. All parts were improvised using scrap materials. The twin engines are old radiator cooler fan motors which I got from the 'Bamboo', a popular area where people buy their 'foreign used' car parts. The gun and lights work, and smoke comes from the funnel. It can be seen on U-Tube. https://www.youtube.com/watch?v=8jEujaAbBR4

Flying model planes was an expensive short-lived hobby. Invariably they would crash in an alligator infested lake near the airfield which we referred to as the 'Bermuda Rectangle'. Retrieving them was a dicey undertaking which I left up to Andrew. He couldn't swim but learned fast.

Chapter 18

———◦———

After sitting our Common Entrance exams I went to QRC (Queen's Royal College). Richard passed for Trinity College, and we drifted apart. That's mainly because he joined the Blue Marlins swim club. There he made a lot of white friends from Shorelands and Bayshore. They called him 'Bugs' (for Bugs Bunny) because of his protruding front teeth.

He once invited me to one of their parties. Every now and then a new dance craze would come out. The latest one was the 'Stones Samba' in which the guys held their testicles while they danced. I quietly sneaked out of there. It wasn't my scene. Later in life he joined the US Air Force as an aircraft engineer. He is based in Iceland and is married to an Icelandic woman.

Richard's older brother, Steve, was a hard case. His parents sent him to Mt. St. Benedict boarding school, hoping the priests would straighten him out. That made it worse since it gave him 'street cred'. He used to start fights over trivial matters. During a cricket match in the street, he once beat up a guy over who should bat next. He made the mistake of picking on some plain clothes cops in Valley Ranch, a nightclub at the end of La Horquette road. They beat him badly and sliced up his face. He still bears the scars.

Kester's brother Stanley lived with him. The two formed a company called Master Marine, and built skies and boats in their shed. Their first boat, named 'She,'capsized on its trial run. The joke ran through the neighborhood - "Look She come! Look She go! Look She sink!" Later Stanley went on to build a beautiful yacht named 'Aura' which is still around. Richard and I would consult him with our models for advice and criticism. He taught me about Navicote, fibreglass and epoxy, which comes in handy to this day.

The Smiths had an apartment which they rented. Once, when I was 17, there was a frustrated divorced woman named Sonja living there with her two daughters. The elder was a pretty 10-year-old named Jenny who loved animals. She used to walk down the street with a large iguana on her head She once asked me for two of my budgies, and I built a cage for her. One day I heard her screaming. I looked through the fence and saw her huddled under the work bench while her mother tried to beat her with a belt. I shouted, "What the hell is wrong with you!"

I went ape-shit and jumped over the fence. She saw me coming and locked herself indoors. All the neighbors came out to see what the commotion was about. The talk went round that Gerry was going to kill Sonja.

I hate all cruelty to children and animals, and it took me a while to simmer down. My mother asked me what I would have done if I'd caught her. I said I'd have wrung her scrawny neck. The dysfunctional family moved out soon afterward.

Many years later I met Jenny, who had grown into a teenaged beauty. I'd gone to a movie with my Dad in Valsayn. After the show, she came over and asked if I could give her a lift. I don't know if she remembered me or was just asking a favor of a perfect stranger. My Dad was impressed, thinking I'd picked up a 'craft'. I dropped her to a party and met her boyfriend who was clearly on drugs. I suspected that she was no better off.

Down the road lived Junior and Michael Reash. Michael, who limed with the older guys, considered himself a 'bad-John' and used to bully Richard and me. One day I devised a scheme to deal with him. Knowing how he liked to fight, we challenged him to a wrestling match. The plan was for him to fight Richard first to put him at ease. Then, when it was my turn, I'd lock his neck and Richard would kick the shit out of him. Just when I was about to start, his mother began calling. Regretfully we had to let him go unscathed. He never knew what an F-up he got away from.

The last house was owned by a decent man named Wilfred. He was a master mason who cast our driveway and did our repairs. He got involved with his pretty young tenant named Cheryl. I believe he went on to become the father of her child. When she dumped him, he came to me sobbing. Imagine me, a young boy, giving advice to a love-sick man 4 times my age. Wilfred eventually died, a broken man, but Cheryl and my Mom remained close friends to the end.

Chapter 19

My 1962 MGB

Across the road was Mrs. Arneaud and her three boys, Charles, Eddie and William. She had a shop and used to make snacks to sell. Once, when she was out, we had a fight in her house using bags of her tamarind balls. The mess was horrific, and we quietly sneaked out before she came home. We used to steal her red mango, which she put on large trays in the sun to cure. That's until we saw a bottle written 'Poison' underneath. It was glacial acetic acid, used as a preservative.

Charles was a bit younger than Richard and me, but 'wotless' enough to be accepted in our posse. His nickname was "Bat Signal" because of the shape made by the gap in his broken front teeth. He loved peanut butter and would open jars in the grocery and scoop it out with his fingers. He'd sample every type, from smooth to extra crunchy. Richard once paid a schoolgirl from Point Cumana 25 cents to have sex with him across the river. She agreed, but he backed out at the last minute because everyone wanted to watch.

Next to them lived Roslyn and her kids, Donna and Junior. 'Rosie' was a tall Venezuelan beauty with fair skin and long black hair. She had gotten married when she was 17 and was now divorced. She wore tight skirts, and every male in the street was smitten by her, including 8 year old me. When she'd walk down the street after work, the cricket match would come to a stop. All the roughneck guys would nod politely and say, "Good evening Miss Roslyn," as she passed. The match would only restart when she reached her house and closed the door.

The only other person to stop a match was a young white girl driving a yellow MG Midget. She was from Newbury Hill and must have gotten the car for her birthday. Cruising down the road, she smiled as she passed the drooling guys. What she didn't know was that we were looking at the car, not at her. I swore I'd own an MG one day. You could keep the girl.

MG stood for 'Morris Garages'. Morris was an English car manufacturer that decided to get into racing to promote their brand. In the early 1920's they brought out a line of beautiful sports cars on which they simply put the letters MG. They were admired for their sleek designs and sporty performance, and hundreds of thousands were sold worldwide. Production stopped in the seventies, but many years later I was able to acquire an old MGB which was built in 1962. With the help of my friend Lenny, an aircraft mechanic, we were able to restore it to its original condition. He worked on the body while I did the mahogany interior. It remains one of my prized possessions.

While spending time in England with Mickhaiel, who was studying medicine at Oxford, I decided to visit the town of Abingdon where the cars were made. I went to a bicycle shop to see if I could rent a bike. Instead of giving me the 10-speed racer I had in mind, the owner brought out a rickety old lady's bicycle which must have been his grandma's. I wondered if it would last the 12 miles to Abingdon and back. It was going to be a long grind. An icy rain was falling and by the time I got there I was wet and frozen. My first action was to get a cup of hot chocolate from a coffee shop to try and thaw out.

The factory no longer existed but I saw the last MGB on the top floor of the town museum. I have no idea how they got it up the narrow stairway. I found the headquarters of the MG club, and met two old timers who used to build the cars. They were amazed that I'd ridden all that way in the rain, and gave me the history of the company. I joined the association which has members all over the world. Few cars invoke such affection, and many of them are still on the road. The brand has been bought out by the SAIC Motor Corporation in China, but the SUVs they make have nothing to do with what an MG is supposed to be.

Chapter 20

Daphne and Major

I was like a big brother to Roslyn's children, Junior and Donna, which she appreciated since their father was never around. I gave them my old toys and used to take them fishing and camping. Once, while camping on an abandoned jetty on Monos Island, Charles got up early to do some fishing. While casting his line the reel flew in the water. He woke up Junior and asked him to get it. Junior refused, saying he didn't want to get wet. Charles picked him up, wrapped in his blanket, and threw him in the sea. He said, "Oh, while you're there, could you get my line?"

My sister Daphne and I adopted their black cocker-spaniel, Major, who had anger management issues. He used to attack the postman, and we got blamed whenever he ripped his pants. He also liked ambushing the chubby paper boy. He'd spring out from the bushes and throw down his bike. The papers would spill and go blowing up the road. That made his day.

He once got run over while chasing a car and was in agony. We took him to a vet in St. James who told us to put warm water on his leg. I wasn't happy with that and carried him to my father's radiology practice. My Dad put him on the table, and with a quick tug, reset his dislocated leg. I was amazed, and never so proud of my Dad.

The family moved to Venezuela when Donna was 11. A few years later, when she was 18, she came back for a brief visit. My mom said she was a stunning beauty, like her mother, and wanted to see me. I had a girlfriend at the time, and kept far. My Mom used to drag Keith and me to church, and I remembered the warning, "lead us not into temptation." Roslyn returned a few years ago and told me that Donna was seriously ill with kidney failure. She needed a transplant, or she would die. With the dire situation in Venezuela, I shudder to think what has become of her.

Chapter 21

Next was the Kumar's, who became the second Indian family on the street. The father was an engineer who helped build the Port of Spain docks. He had 3 daughters who were older than me, and I never got to know them very well. They invited me to a birthday party once and I sat and ate the entire plate of wafers on the table. Sixty years later the sight or smell of a waver makes me nauseous.

They were the first people on the street to own a TV, a 13- inch black and white Zenith. Every night the 'homies' on the block would drop in their living room to watch TTT until it signed off. Mr. Kumar would leave the front door open for them and go to sleep. They would lock it on their way out. This shows how different we lived in those days.

Next were the Steven sisters, Gladys and Gloria. They were middle-aged off-white women with irritating high-pitched voices. The way they cackled you'd swear they had a poultry depot in the back. We used to write anonymous love letters and stuff them in their mailbox. They were very catholic, and one ended up marrying a priest. My mom said that, when she went with them to harvests in the rural areas, the villagers would supply young girls for 'the holy fathers'.

They lived with their grandmother, who was 100. One night, while she was in her driveway, Keith tested a homemade rocket. It went up and came back down, heading straight for the old lady. Seeing an unguided missile streaking towards her she started to run in slow motion. It whizzed over her head, missing her by inches. She died soon after.

Next were the Cumberbatches, Uncle George and Auntie Lilly, two sweet elderly people. Their son John had a pituitary condition which caused him to grow to almost 7 feet. As such we called him 'Bamboo'. He was a popular guy and became a radio sports commentator. Later in life he became an alcoholic and died prematurely.

Next were the Kings, another bi-racial family. Auntie Doris, an American, was a sweet person who had room in her heart for everyone. I still

use one of her expressions - "I see, said the blind man." Richard and
would wait outside her kitchen window every morning for breakfast
which her youngest son, William gave trouble to eat. She'd sit him on her
lap with a belt, but it did no good. Eventually she'd give up and pass the
food through the window for us. Pancakes, hash browns and maple syrup
were unheard of in our homes, so that was a treat.

Their father, Uncle Chris, was an imposing man who owned a con-
tracting firm. He used to have rowdy card games with his workmen every
Friday night in his garage. My father once mentioned to him that I'd done
badly in the test. He called me into his room and gave me a stern lecture.
He told me about a guy who failed his exams but went on to become
an Industrial Court judge. Who does that with other people's kids these
days?

William was close to my brother Keith. Even at the age of six he had a
charge account at the Ross's drugstore behind our house. We'd 'persuade'
him to buy us sweets and ice cream until his mom saw the bills. The
whole family, including their other children Carol, Christopher and Cheryl, moved to NY. Most of them got jobs with Pan Am Airlines. When
William would come to visit, he'd have to take back a case of bottled red
Solo soft drinks and a bunch of uncut coconuts for his father. His suitcase weighed a ton. It shows how Trinis miss their home, their food and
their culture.

Chapter 22

Next were the Ferrieras. I didn't know old Uncle Hugh very well but had more dealings with his wife, Auntie Grace. She used to sew the sails for our model yachts. One day she asked Charles and me to pick some sapodillas from her tree. We filled a box for her, and she took out two small ones and gave them to us. We got pissed and decided to fix that.

The next day I climbed the tree and threw down sapodillas for Charles, who was catching below. The rain started to fall, and the tree got so slippery I couldn't move. Charles, realizing I was stuck, started yelling "Tief, Tief," and ran off with the bag. Grace opened her upstairs window and caught me red- handed. She didn't make a fuss, but I swore I'd get back at Charles for that.

A few days later I heard his mother calling for him. I hopped on my bike, rode down the road and told her that Charles said he wasn't coming. He said he'd take the licks instead. She said, "Is that so!", and went inside for the belt. Later, when Charles breezed in, his mother said, "So you go take the licks, eh?" and started blazing his tail.

The Ferrieras used to rent an annex behind their house to an American woman. She had a young son named Jack who played with us. After dropping him at school, a guy named Mr. Gudger would come and visit her. Richard, who knew more about these things, figured that something fishy was going on. Her windows were frosted so he couldn't see through. This had him quite frustrated.

One day, after she left to drop Jack, he persuaded me to come with him and hide in the room. I slipped into the closet while Richard crawled under the bed. He wanted to be close in on the action. It wasn't long before the mother and Mr. Gudger came in and started doing their thing. I got a bird's eye view, but Richard couldn't see squat. His head was also getting banged up by the action. He started crawling out from below the bed till his face was right between them. That's when Gudger saw him. He grabbed him by the neck and started to cuss. By then I'd seen enough for one day and figured it was time to leave. I came bursting out of the cupboard and all hell broke loose. I was out of there in a flash, leaving Richard to sort things out. Not my circus – not my monkeys.

Next were the Miles – Ruby and her daughter Gene Gene Miles was a well- known model and celebrity. She was a voluptuous off-white woman who tantalized every man, including my father, who would salivate when she walked down the road.

She worked as a clerk at the Factory Inspectorate and became aware of a racket involving the granting of gas station licenses. Her testimony at the Commission of Enquiry resulted in the firing of the factory inspector. In doing so she stepped on some big political corns. She was slandered and dismissed from the public service without benefits. Deeply humiliated, she started drinking and became a hopeless alcoholic. She died in her sleep of heart complications at age 42.

She is now associated with those who have suffered character assassination, social ostracism, depression and death as a result of the stand they take against government corruption.

Gene Miles (1930 1972)

64

Chapter 23

The next street was called Strathaven Avenue. At the top lived the Johnsons. They had a son named Hadyn, who had Down syndrome. The older boys would 'take advantage' of him, pulling down his pants and teasing him. We let him lime with us even though he couldn't speak properly. His only conversation with me was, "Ay Gerry, wuz yer name?" I felt sorry for him because his father used to beat him mercilessly. I think he was ashamed of him since his other children were normal and bright. At age twelve he drowned while bathing at the Yacht Club. Some say he committed suicide. Either way I think it was a blessing.

The only people we had much to do with on Second Street were the Hendersons who lived at the end. We were close because their mother, Auntie Joyce, and my Mom were good friends. It was a big wild family. Their father, Uncle Douglas, owned a betting shop in St. James. He was into cock fighting, which was illegal, and had pens in his yard with the most beautiful birds. I think he treasured them more than his wayward children.

He had a girlfriend, Auntie Jean, whom he moved into the house. I don't know how Joyce felt about her being there, but she never showed any animosity. She was into something called metaphysics, a branch of philosophy that studied the fundamental nature of reality. I guess that gave her the strength to deal with the situation. When the family moved to England they got divorced and he married Jean.

The eldest son was Michael, 19, who was our 'El Padrone'. There was a large black family called the Raymonds who lived up the road. One of them threatened to beat us up. We told Michael, who took his pellet gun and strode into their yard. He warned the eldest that if any one of them interfered with us he would shoot him between the eyes. We never had trouble with them again.

His younger sister Patricia, 18, was a very attractive tomboy. She did fencing and had a black belt in Judo. She and her brothers practiced sword fighting, using real swords. No one messed with her. Once I rode into their garage where a dart game was in progress. They continued playing and a dart got stuck in my head. They pulled it out and everyone was fascinated to see the hole it made.

Next was Ronnie, 17 - a very decent handsome guy. He and his younger brother Jimmy were very religious. They attended the Seventh Day Adventist College in Maracas Valley. Ronnie went on to become a priest, and managed to bring God into every conversation. They used to have Western-style gunfights across the river, using their BB guns. My Mom often had to remove pellets from their skin. Because she worked as a radiographer in the hospital, she was the closest thing to a nurse.

They once made a raft out of bamboo. When the river came down in flood, they launched it and jumped on. They were swept out to sea and were rescued by fishermen the next day.

Next was Reggie 15, who was intelligent and introverted. He was given a large chemistry set for his birthday which he used to concoct explosives. The neighbors used to complain about the pyrotechnics emanating from their yard. Once, while bursting bamboo, the blast blew off his eyebrows. He came by my mom to pick the carbide out of his eyes.

Then there was David, 11, who was my dear friend. He was a quiet, thoughtful guy and we got along well. He had a bike and taught me to ride. When I asked my father to get me one, he said I'd have to pass my Common Entrance exam first. With my Dad there was no such thing as a free ride. As soon as I got my results, I dragged him to Fuller's on Henry Street and showed him the bike I wanted. It was a metallic blue Raleigh racer with chrome fenders. He was reluctant because of the narrow wheels, but I insisted. I'd been drooling over that bike for a long time, and didn't want the Humber postman's model he preferred. He relented and I sprang on the saddle and rode all the way home to St. Joseph.

For the next 7 years, until I got my license, it would be my mode of transport and source of independence. It was eventually stolen outside the oval where I went to see a cricket match. I'd parked against the wall where a policeman was on duty. I figured it would be safe. When I came back the bike and the cop were gone. I'm not implying anything, but say, "tief" and I'll whistle.

Many years later, Shaheeba and I met David and his lovely French fiancée' in London. They took us for a walk in the park and offered us something to eat. That sounded great since I was hungry. We'd had lunch at a Lebanese restaurant, and the expensive quail I ordered looked like a fried-dry day-old chick. David's 'meal' turned out to be two digestive biscuits. We thanked them kindly, realizing it was what they could afford.

The last child was Jason, 5, who was the wildest. If he came at you with a knife you'd better run because he would use it. He used to beg the garbage men for cigarettes and smoke them under his bed. He was the runt of the litter, and we figured that smoking stunted his growth. I was shocked when I heard that he too become a priest.

Their parents were never around, but they had a maid who was supposed to do the cooking. All she ever made were big jugs of Milo, which was what they lived on. After drinking their fill they would lie on the ground, lift up their shirts and compare the size of their bellies. We all had bottles of mercury which we played with. Looking back, I think it affected our brains.

On Thursday nights we'd all go to the movies. The StarLite drive-in cinema in nearby Diego Martin had a special offer of 'Two Dollars a Car Load.' Mike and Ronnie would take us to see a 'double' in two cars. When we got there all thirteen of us would pile into Joyce's old Peugeot.

There was a 'sleeping policeman' just before the toll booth. The car was so heavy that some of us would have to get out and push it over the hump. This was done in full view of the ticket attendant. He'd just shake his head and collect the $2. During the movie, we'd buy a plate of chips to share with everyone. We couldn't afford the chicken.

Their neighbor across the road had a son named Earnest. I once heard him calling out, "Mommie, can have my half of apple now?" I thought that was pathetic. I vowed that, if I ever had children, they would have a whole apple and could eat it whenever they wanted. Right now my two parrots, puffy and stuffy, are munching on my apples.

Next to them lived the Butchers. Their eldest son, Ray, went on to become a Coast Guard captain. He once intercepted a Venezuelan trawler fishing in our waters. He lined up the crew and beat them with a king fish. He was later charged with assault and battery. I believe the case was thrown out by the magistrate because his attorney argued that a fish is not a deadly weapon.

Speaking of magistrates, I nearly got arrested once. I'd gone to work and parked in my usual spot at the airport. I didn't know it had been converted into a 'No Parking' zone, and was given a ticket by the Airport Authority security guard. I asked a friend where I had to pay the fine. He said, "Go to the magistrate's court in Arima. You'll see a guy in a cage. Pay him the money and he'll give you a receipt."

I went the next day when the court was in session. The magistrate was a big black woman who resembled a post-menopausal bull frog. Surely enough there was a cage at the side of the court with a guy inside. I asked him if this was where you paid the fines. He said yes, and pocketed the money. Just then the frog turned and saw me. She exclaimed, "Who's that talking to the prisoner? Constable, arrest him!" As I saw the big burly policeman approaching, I used my well-practiced routine and GTFOH (Get the fuck outta here).

Chapter 24

My first kindergarten was a private catholic school run by a stern old man who beat the children with a tamarind whip. He must have realized that mora was no good. We had to say a lot of prayers, and I wondered why this poor lady named Mary was full of grease.

Later I went to another pre-school, along with my father's youngest half- brother, Godfrey. He was just a few years older and enjoyed shooting people with his rubber-band sling shot. He always had a bag of ammo which he made by tearing pages from his copy books. He would buy us Kool-Aid 'ice blocks' from Miss Mary, the Chinese lady who had a parlor on the corner. He was a fat funny guy and we loved him dearly.

At five years old I finally went to a proper school, Tranquility Government Boys Intermediate School. My kindergarten teacher was a dear old lady named Miss James. Once I put my pocket money penny down my socks and forgot it was there. When recess came, I couldn't find it and told Miss James. She gave me five cents, more money than I'd ever seen. I was able to buy an ice-cream Jell-it instead of the usual cheap popsicle.

My first taste of embarrassment occurred in her class. To look taller, my friends and I decided to sit on our book bags. One of them asked me what I had for lunch, and I told him a banana. That's when I remembered that the soft ripe banana was in the bag I was sitting on! I opened the bag, and it was not a pretty sight. Banana pulp had squeezed between the pages of my books. I had to go outside and wash the bag under the standpipe. Despite Miss James's attempts to maintain order, everyone crowded by the door squealing with laughter.

I also learned my first joke.

"Why are there no phones in China?"

"That's because there's so many 'Wings' and 'Wongs' they 'fraid they wing the wong number."

I still think it's funny, but I guess it would be considered politically incorrect now.

I can remember all my teachers but have forgotten some of their names. That includes my standard two teacher who had a habit of rapping students on the knuckles with a triangular ruler. He once tried it with me but no way I was allowing that. My father was a radiologist, and I told him if he broke my knuckles he'd have to pay for the X-ray. He cracked up and let me go. Over the years, whenever he saw me, he'd say "Barrow, you'll really make me pay for the X-Ray?"

Chapter 25

An important part of school days was the things we did at recess. These included pitching marbles, racing jockeys, flying chicky-chongs and spinning tops. Since you look confused, I'll expatiate.

'Canal jockeys' were wooden rafts made from popsicle sticks. They were about one inch long and carved by scraping the wood against the road. The usual designs were oval or diamond shapes. These were placed in a canal where the water would move them along. I usually won because I'd rub the underside of my jockey with candle wax to make it smooth and slippery.

'Spinning top' was a necessary skill when growing up. Tops were usually made of guava wood and a 4 -inch nail, sharpened to a point. Those who didn't have an uncle with carpentry skills had to buy the cheap red and blue ones from Miss Mary. These didn't last long since the object of the game was to 'jig', or break the other person's top by hitting it with your own, hence the sharpened nail. That's why guava wood was the material of choice. It was indestructible.

I can still spin a top today, but never learned to do any of the fancy tricks, like catching them in my hand. I now enjoy making them in my workshop out of various colorful woods like samaan, teak and mahogany. Check out my U- Tube video 'Top Spin' to see how. https://www.youtube.com/watch?v=- FiSMLiQkI0.

I spray them with several coats of polyurethane varnish, mount them on a driftwood base and give them as gifts. I made one for my wife, the Hospital Medical Director, to put on her desk. It's labeled 'Top Dog'.

Slingshots were made from the 'Y' of guava branches and the inner tube of bicycle tires. These required less skill to construct, and most boys made their own. They were used for shooting doves and keskidees but were not very accurate. Birds didn't mind, once you were aiming at them. The stone 'bullets' were held in place with a flap of canvas cut from the 'tongue' of your Bata 'Jim Boots'. We all got into trouble by cutting our shoes and stealing our father's bicycle tubes.

Chicky-chongs were small kites made from a sheet of copy-book paper. A second page was torn in a spiral to make the tail. Unlike larger kites, these had no 'compass' to keep them at the correct angle of attack. You had to run and pull them to keep them aloft. Proper kites were made from colored kite paper and 'cocoyea' stalks, held together with thread and a paste made from flour and water. A long length of expired type-writer ribbon was used for the tail.

Guys would stick broken glass or razors on their tails, using a tree sap called 'lagley', to cut each other's thread. A cut kite was said to 'io' as it drifted away. Lagley was also spread on the tree branches to catch song-birds like semps and picoplats. Having a bird in a wooden cage is still a popular hobby and it isn't unusual to see big men walking around with their tiny pets.

Large kites were called 'mad bulls' and required skills passed down through generations. They came in various designs and colors depending on the builder. A thick string called marlin was needed when flying them since the forces involved were immense. They had two tails made of cotton and were beautiful to watch. During the 'kite season', from February to April when the trade winds blew, you'd often see these beautiful kites high up over the savannah.

'Pitch' was another game, using marbles. There was 'three hole', and another called 'rings' in which each person placed his marbles in a ring drawn in the dirt. Any marble you knocked out was yours to keep. As with any form of gambling, this led to frequent altercations. Your favorite marble was called a 'taw'. The double sized marble was known as 'big unks'. The object of some games involved trying to shatter your opponent's taw. For this reason, some boys used large steel ball bearings known as 'slugs'. Those who lost a game would have their knuckles rapped with a marble. This was known as a 'bokie'. Getting a bokie from a slug or a big unks was not a pleasant experience.

'Schooch' was a game where you ran around trying to hit others with a 'wind ball' or bean bag filled with tamarind seeds. In QRC, to make it interesting, we used a 'cork ball' which resulted in bruised backs and a

The most dangerous game was called 'raising'. Guys would stand in a ring and kick a small rubber ball which you had to keep bouncing. The game was played in the canteen at lunchtime and the whole school would gather round to watch. It was hazardous because anyone who missed the ball would get 'hailed' by the crowd. Hailing meant having your head pounded by everyone. Running didn't help since you'd be chased and caught. It was a very intense, stressful activity and I never got involved. I may be ignorant but I'm not stupid.

There were no toy shops in those days so we had to devise our own equipment. You could make a gun from two clothes pins and use it to shoot small stones. A blow gun was made from a plastic ball point pen with the ink cartridge removed. This could be used to shoot rice grains. A 'zwill' was made by flattening a crown cork and punching two holes in the center. By threading a piece of twine through the holes and winding it up you could get it to spin very fast. I used to make mine from a Milo tin cover, in which I cut teeth. This acted like a buzz saw.

Another common toy was a 'tractor' made with an empty thread bob-bin, a rubber band and a washer made of candle. These moved slowly and could climb a slope. The simplest toy was rolling a bicycle rim with a stick. I used an old car tire which I rolled with my hand. As usual, I did my own thing.

The most popular game was 'cock fighting'. That's when guys would jump on the backs of their friends and try to kick down the other teams. I wonder if that's still played today. Other boys would tie knots in the tall grass to trip others when they were running. Shaheeba's father was the principal of the TML Muslim school. I'm told he once caught a guy tying knots and made him run through them. Past pupils said he was 'dredo', but I found him to be a most pleasant person.

Probably the most obscure activity was 'fishing' for worms. You'd take a grass stalk and put it down a narrow worm hole. The worm would bite the stalk and you'd pull it out. You'd then put the worm in an ant's nest and see it contort while being bitten. I'm fairly sure the present genera-tion has no clue what I'm talking about.

Chapter 26

At recess everyone crowded around 'Shakey, who sold aloo (potato) pies for a penny each. These were round and a lot smaller than the ones sold today. All the vendors who sold aloo were called 'Shakey'. That's because of the rocking motion they made as they hurriedly cut the pies to add a dash of pepper and mango chutney. These pies have completely disappeared, replaced by 'doubles,' our national breakfast.

There were many other interesting things to eat, like snatty dongs, balata, chilli bibbi, gru-gru bev, fried channa, sugar cake, benny balls and toolum. These were incredibly cheap. You could get three red and yellow 'paradise plum' sweets for one cent. That would cost a dollar now, assuming you can find them. My favorite snacks were guava sweets. These were red crudely shaped sugary balls with a matchstick stuck inside.

I used to wait in my father's office after school while he finished reading his X-rays. A nurse would bring him a glass of orange juice which he would let me have. I would always leave some for him. I wanted to become a radiologist just to get free juice. I also enjoyed looking at the films to see how much stool was in the bowels.

One evening he was running late and gave me 50 cents to buy a rock cake and a soft drink from across the road. Instead, I blew it all on guava sweets. While driving home he saw me sucking something and asked what was in the bag. I said guava sweets and showed him my stash. He grabbed the bag and threw it out the window saying, "Are you mad? Your teeth would fall out like rain!" An old lady from Toco, who apparently supplied the country, died, and they are no longer available. I've since taught myself to make them, so I have a steady supply.

My favorite fruit was tonka bean. This was a brown oval-shaped fruit with a thin leathery skin. Below this was a layer of pulp on a large seed. You ate the pulp by scraping it off with your teeth. You'd then wash the seed and put it to dry. The seed was covered with a layer of yellow fur which you could use as a powder puff. Alternately you could draw a mouth, eyes and nose to make a face. The inside of the seeds had pods used to make vanilla essence.

At recess, kids usually bought a 'press'. This was shaved ice, molded into a conical shape, and dipped into red and yellow guava syrup. Condensed milk could be added at extra cost. There were no sanitary 'sno-cone' cups in those days - you held the cold dripping thing in your hands.

One friend of mine got his press late because of the long line. When the bell rang there was no way he was going to dump it. Instead, he put it in his shirt pocket and went to class. Every now and then he'd take it out, give it a slurp and put it back. I don't even want to think about that mess. It was a common practice to 'borrow' someone's chewing gum, chew it for a while, then give it back. For me, that was going too far. Take my gum if you want but keep it to yourself.

There were two old ladies who sold snacks from glass cases. One of them had massive tamarind balls which she sold for a penny, an extravagance at the time. The talk went round that she rolled them with her foot, so everyone kept away. I once saw a girl buying one and was horrified. I warned her about it, and she immediately dropped it on the ground. The next day, as I was running past, the woman called out to me saying, "What did you say to that girl?" I continued running as if I hadn't heard, but realized I may have done something wrong. From that day I learned a lesson about not listening to rumors, but getting the facts before coming to a conclusion.

Chapter 27

The standard 3 teacher, Mrs. Roach, was a nasty piece of work. She was a big strong woman who resembled a rhinoceros, both in shape and temperament. Her husband was involved with another teacher, so she took out her frustrations on her students. She would beat the entire class just to achieve harmony. I got my first taste of her medieval malevolence on my second day in her class. She said, "All those who didn't do their homework, line up in front. Homework? Good lord, who the F gives homework on the first day?

I stood at the end of the line with six other trembling wimps. She started from a side.

"Why didn't you do your homework?" "Miss I forgot"

"Oh, you forgot? I will fix your memory. Stay right there." The next guy claimed he was sick.

She said "Wait till I finish with you - you will need an ambulance. Remain there."

Each guy came up with a more creative excuse, including a power cut, flash flood, a dog eating his book, and the train having a flat tire. All to no avail.

I was last and realized I had to come up with something original. The usual stuff wasn't cutting it.

When asked, I told her that the previous teacher never gave homework, so I wasn't accustomed....

"Wait!" she interrupted. "You blaming the other teacher for not doing your homework? The rest of you sit down."

Needless to say, I got it for all six, who were happy to spectate.

Roachie used to beat for the slightest infraction. If the class was noisy, She'd beat for spelling errors, sweaty backs and inky hands. This was hard to avoid in the hot sun, and because she insisted that we write with fountain pens. The only pens we could afford were the cheap Chinese ones that used to leak. She didn't want to see any cross-outs or erasures. Someone asked her what to do if we made a mistake. She said, "make a what?"

Beating children had a therapeutic effect on her, and she had her favorites. First was Aboud, a fat Syrian boy who used to sweat a lot. She would beat him if his shirt was wet. He would spend his lunch period in the shade of the bicycle shed but it didn't help. The thought of getting licks made him perspire more.

Then there was Stimson, whose father owned a funeral agency. She enjoyed beating him because of the way he jumped around like a horse. That provided her with sport and entertainment. She would say, "Stimson, ah go bury ya today," before starting the blows.

She once got a cane from somewhere down south which she soaked in brine for three days. It seems the tamarind and guava whips were not hacking it. They shattered too easily. The cane was flexible and would last longer. After school, Richard and I picked the lock on her cupboard door and took the cane home. We chopped it into small pieces, burned it with kerosene and buried the ashes in an unmarked grave. No way she was using that on us.

The most feared rod in the school belonged to the 5th-standard teacher, Mr. Stanford. He got a piece of mahogany from a sawmill, then shaped and varnished it into a thing of beauty. It resembled a billiards cue. On the handle he engraved the words 'The Tickler', a reference to something in Dickens I was unfamiliar with.

Once, after a particularly grave offence, probably getting a sum wrong, Mrs. R sent a boy for the Tickler. When she was finished with him, she had reduced the fine piece of furniture to splinters. When he returned the remains to its owner he said, "She broke this on you?" "Yes sir," said the hapless boy. "My good whip!" said Stanford and started to blaze the boy with his belt.

There was one guy named Marlon who seemed impervious to pain. He said he put his hands on a hot iron each night to toughen them. The rest of us simply wore three layers of jockey shorts.

Years later I used to ride home from QRC on my bike. I knew she lived in St. James which was on my route. I always hoped I'd see her crossing the road so I could knock her down and say, "Oopsie". While all the teachers administered corporal punishment, she went too far.

I saw a headline in the papers recently where a parent was taking legal action against the Ministry because a teacher slapped his child. My, how things have changed. In our day the child would have gotten more licks when he got home.

I was told a story by a friend who was in our class. He said that one of our classmates, Anthony, who's now an eminent cardiologist, noticed her in hospital while doing his ward rounds. He checked her chart and saw her condition. He leaned over her and said, "Miss Roach, you remember me?" She opened her eyes and said, "Tony, is that you?" He said, "Yes Miss, and I just want to tell you, you go dead". I don't know if this story is true but that's what I heard.

After her class, I got skipped to 5th standard. I was happy for that since the 4th standard teacher, Mr. Lynch, who used to scratch his balls at assembly, kept a length of multi-core telephone cable on his desk. I don't know what he used it for, but I didn't want to find out.

Chapter 29

Daphne, aged 7

Standard Five was the "Common Entrance" class. That's when you were prepared to write the Eleven Plus Exam. Mr. Williams was an excellent teacher, but the amount of Mathematics and English Grammar involved was immense. This has been replaced by the SEA (Secondary Entrance Assessment), supposedly to reduce the stress, but the object is still the same. You have to pass with a 98% average to get into one of the 'prestige' colleges. That could affect your future since there is an immense difference between the government secondary and denominational schools. For parents who face this pressure, it is an effective form of birth control.

In Port of Spain the first choices were QRC (Queens Royal College), CIC (College of the Immaculate Conception) and Fatima College, the latter two being catholic. To help me prepare, my brother and I moved from Glencoe to live with my father in St. Joseph. This was a significant change in our lives.

To say we were not happy there would be an understatement. We referred to it as Stalag 13, after the POW camp in the TV series 'Hogan's heroes'. Elizabeth Gardens, St. Joseph, was a new development with few houses. We were surrounded by bush. We missed our friends and our carefree way of life. Living with my Dad meant there were rules, restrictions and chores, a seismic shock for us. I also didn't get along with his new wife Rita, mainly because I was a 'harden' and rebellious SOB. My poor Dad was caught between a rock and a hard place 'parting fight' between two of us. Our only relief from this restrictive regimen would be on weekends when he would take us out to fly our planes, sail our boats, collect seashells or go fishing. I think it was a welcome break for him too.

It was worse for my sister Daphne, who was shipped off to boarding school in England at the tender age of ten. Trinidad was a British colony at the time, so those who could afford it did what the English did - off-load their children.

Daphne hated her time there with passion. She was very close to my Dad and felt abandoned. When she returned to live with my mother at age thirteen, she was a social and educational misfit. Not having sat Common Entrance she could not be placed in a government school. As such she was shuffled around various private schools where she met and associated with the Americans.

These were the kids of US servicemen who were stationed at the US Naval base in Chaguaramus, part of the Lend-Lease act of 1941. Having fair skin, she was accepted by this clan. Living amongst the English and Americans, she began to identify herself more as being white rather than Indian. This caused a life-long rift with my mother who expected her to be a traditional 'batee', baking sada roti and roasting baigan.

With each change in school Daphne fell back a year. She then quit school entirely without writing her O-Level exams. She became a flight attendant with LIAT and moved to Barbados. By this time she was a perfect stranger to Keith and me, still doing hard time in St. Joseph.

Chapter 29

Keith and I slept on one bed and had to share an old threadbare blanket. The nights up on the hill were cold so we'd each try to hog as much of the blanket as possible. To do this we'd roll it around ourselves and pull. Eventually the blanket succumbed to our efforts. It split down the middle, sending us flying off the bed. That resolved any further conflict, since now we each had our own piece of blanket.

Sometimes there'd be a storm at night, with the wind blowing the rain through the windows. Instead of closing them we'd just hide under the covers. It was like camping. We didn't consider St. Joseph to be our home so didn't give a shit. My Dad would come to wake us for school the next morning and find the room under an inch of water. He'd ask angrily, "Didn't you know it was raining?" Rain? No, we were fast asleep.

Keith was sickly with asthma and was also accident prone. Once while we were burning rubbish in the back yard, he began poking it with a stick. I don't know how it happened, but he somehow fell in the fire, burning his shins.

On another occasion, while on vacation on Chacachacare, an island near Venezuela, he fell and broke his arm. 'Chac' was a leper colony at the time and had a hospital. My Dad took him for an X-Ray only to find that the machine hadn't worked for several months. Being who he was, he had it up and running in no time, to the amazement of the staff.

Keith and I were partners in crime. We had our ups and downs but always came together during an emergency. One interesting incident occurred when he was roasting cashew nuts in the bedroom. While lying on the bed he cooked them one at a time by holding them over a candle using a pair of pliers. This was too slow a process, so he decided to speed things up.

He got an empty paint tin and filled it with dry leaves and twigs. He placed the cashew nuts on top and lit the bundle. At first things went well until the cashews ignited. They began to emit jets of flammable gas, like mini flame throwers. The whole thing erupted like napalm in the room, setting the curtains alight. To save the house we threw buckets of water on the flames. This caused huge clouds of smoke to rise, blackening the walls and ceiling.

We had to move fast since my Dad would be back soon. While we never got licks from him, we didn't want chance it. You can push a good man only so far. We scrubbed the walls, repainted the ceiling and cut away the burnt edges of the curtains. No one ever noticed a thing, including the fact that the curtains were now a lot shorter.

Another mishap occurred when we accidentally demolished his orchid house. Our house was on a hill with a yard which sloped steeply. My father, who was an avid orchid and cactus collector, built a greenhouse at the bottom of the hill to house his plants. With no friends to play with, Keith and I had to improvise our entertainment. We came up with an idea for a game. He would roll a car tire from the top of the slope, and I would catch it at the bottom. It seemed reasonable at the time, even though it was raining.

As it came bounding down the hill the tire picked up incredible speed. It also became wet and slippery. I tried my best to stop it but couldn't. It crashed into the orchid house, smashing everything in sight. The scene of devastation resembled the LA earthquake, but on a grander scale. Once again, we had to move fast before my Dad came home. Fortunately, we used to help him 'pot' the plants and knew how. That involved placing the orchids in clay pots and securing them with pieces of broken brick and charcoal. We thought we did a bang-up job, but my Dad took one look and wanted to know what happened. As usual, we knew nothing.

We also had two pet chickens. Day-old chicks, dyed in various colors, were distributed at a children's Easter function at the StarLite Drive-in. We got a couple, and I built a coup for them out of scrap wood. Each morning before school Keith and I would let them loose to roam around the yard. In the evening we would have to catch them, which wasn't easy. Chickens can't fly but can run very fast. Karen and Billy would peep out through their bedroom window and squeal with laughter as we chased them around the yard. I fed them with 'growing mash', and they grew to an enormous size.

One evening we came back from school, and they were nowhere to be found. My Dad, who loved to cook, announced that we were having 'chicken steaks' for dinner. I suspected fowl play and refused to eat any.

Chapter 30

Queens Royal College

Despite these minor distractions, I passed my CE exam for Fatima College. I wasn't entirely pleased since that was my third choice. I persuaded my father to pull some strings and get me transferred to Queens Royal College. All my male relatives had gone there, plus I didn't want to go to a school with a silly name like Fatima. Who was 'Fatima' anyway?

On the first day of college we wore our dress uniform, which included grey trousers, khaki socks, white shirt, striped tie and a navy-blue blazer. As was the tradition, my friends and I went back to Tranquility to show off. Mr. Williams, who only months before blazed us for being 'dotish', paraded us in front the class as shining examples of intellect and scholarship. Unfortunately, that dress uniform is no longer in use.

The QRC principal at the time was Mr. Laltoo, affectionately known as 'The Lal'. Though short and round in stature, he was universally feared and respected. Once, as was often the case, we had a free period with no supervision. Some guys at the back started a poker game, using real money. It was then that the Lal entered the room. The ones who saw him immediately brought out their Spanish books and pretended to be vocab. However, one miserable fellow named Gosine, whose back was to the door, didn't notice his presence. He continued dealing cards while smoking a funny looking cigarette. Sensing that something was amiss he glanced up and saw the Lal glaring down at him. He took a long, last drag of his joint, stumped it out and followed the principal to his office for a caning.

For a really serious transgression a master would send a student for the 'Black Book'. He would enter the offence and the boy would have to take it back to the office. Depending on what was written the Lal would some-times cane the offender over the PA system. Most guys would walk slowly around the building a few times before handing in the book, hoping, like a boxer, to be saved by the bell.

I firmly believe that the fortunes of a school lie entirely with the principal. In those days you had Fr. Lai Fook in CIC, Anna Mahase in SAGHS, Miss Shurland in Bishops, Mrs.Valere in St. Francois... These were not people you trifled with. Keith went to Trinity, and they were intimidated by their principal, Mr. Phelps. It was rumored he was a tank commander who fought against Rommel at Tobruk.

I asked Keith, "Does he beat people?"

"No"

"Does he shout at you?"

"No"

"What does he do?"

"He *looks* at you."

Chapter 31

Gerry with calypso legend Lord

When I entered QRC in 1965 it was the top school in the country. We won the Jerningham Medal, which is now called the President's Medal. The names of these 'Island Schol' winners were painted on the walls of the assembly hall, going back a century. When Mr. Laltoo left, he was replaced by a string of jokers who no one respected. Like the West Indies cricket team, we declined from being on top to becoming an embarrassment.

Speaking of cricket, I would skip classes to go see my 'Windies' heroes at the Queen's Park Oval. A 'nutsman' named Jumbo would pass around the stands selling nuts for one dollar. With his trademark cry, "Allya look it here, ah have it," he'd throw bags of nuts at customers with unerring accuracy. The money would be handed down through the crowd.

I sometimes had the privilege of operating the scoreboard during Test matches. I managed the 'Fall of Wickets' – the only job they trusted me with. As such I was able to admire the majesty of Garfield Sobers and Frank Worrell, the flair of Rohan Kanhai, the guile of Lance Gibbs and the intimidating pace of Wes Hall and Charlie Griffith.

We got even better under Clive Lloyd. Our innings would start with Desmond Haynes and Gordon Greenidge, our two openers. They would put down a century each, just to get the board ticking. Then, when you thought it was safe, in came Viv Richards, followed by Richie Richardson, Gus Logie, Larry Gomes and Lloyd himself. There'd be 500 runs on the board by tea. Once, during a match against England, a white woman took off her clothes and streaked across the field. She jumped over the stumps, hoping to disrupt our batsmen's concentration. It didn't work. Gus and Larry put down another fifty.

I felt sorry for the English and Aussie captains who were 'Black Washed' repeatedly. When they came into bat, they faced the wrath of Michael Holding, Joel Garner, Colin Croft and Andy Roberts, - the Four Horsemen of the Apocalypse.

The only team to weather the onslaught were the Indians, especially their opening batsman, Sunil Gavascar. Lord Relator, in his iconic calypso sang, "You know the West Indies couldn't out Gavascar at all," which was true. I don't bother to follow WI cricket anymore. Defeat is one thing – disgrace is another.

I remain a fan of 'ole time kaiso', true calypso music which no longer exists. This has been replaced by soca, supposedly a blend of soul and calypso. It's neither of them, just senseless party noise. As a boy I used to enjoy going to the calypso tents and listen to the witty compositions of greats like Sparrow, Bomber and Explainer, just to name a few. These were brilliant people, who, given a proper education, could have been rocket scientists. Their songs were filled with double entendre, such as 'The Whip' and 'Iron Man', by Zandolie. My favorite is 'What a slippers doing under meh bed?' by Penguin. Even though most of them have passed, much of their music has been preserved on U-Tube.

I also love the sound of a steel pan, especially when played on its own. However, I find the arrangements played at the Panorama Competition to be too intricate and convoluted. We no longer have Lord Kitchener to write tuneful compositions. Surprisingly I'm not into Carnival, said to be the greatest show on Earth. That's mainly because I don't drink and have no interest in baking in the hot sun. I once tried chipping in a band on Carnival Tuesday. The sight of round naked bottoms bumping in my face did nothing for my hypertension.

Chapter 32

My first 5 years in college were abysmal, to put it mildly. At that time the government had just opened the many junior and senior secondary schools and poached the colleges for teachers. I was in the 'B' stream and was taught by ex A-Level students. We gave these rookie teachers a hard time. One trick was to quickly shift around our desks when their backs were turned. That confused them since they had a chart with names and places. There was once a person named Alexander who was supposed to join the class but never did. During roll call someone at the back would say, "present" when his name was called. It was several months before our form master realized that Alexander didn't exist.

The biggest instigator in these shenanigans was my cousin, Robbie v. Our balding Spanish teacher, who we called 'Beligrafo' (a willful distortion of the correct Spanish word for ball point pen) because of his big belly, once told Robbie, "Boy, I have more brains in my big toe than you have in your head." Robbie replied, "Yes sir, that may be true, but I have more hair on my big toe than you have on your head."

We used to 'break biche' (cut classes) to go and see movies that were restricted to 18 years and over. We'd hop on our bikes during lunch break and watch a 12:30 'double'. In those days you always got two movies for the price of one. We never paid a cent. We realized that the ticket collector for 'pit' usually left the box once the movie started. We'd just wait a couple minutes then slip in for free. It also negated the fact that we were only 11 years old. These Swedish soft porn movies were disguised as medical documentaries. 'Helga', for example, dealt with natural childbirth. Instead of being aroused, everyone was disgusted.

'Pit' was the front section of the cinema, which was the cheapest. It cost only 55 cents to get in. The disadvantage was that you got a stiff neck from sitting below the screen. I liked going there because of the colorful characters who frequented it. There'd be lively 'picong' which was often more entertaining than the show. Once there was a baby crying in the back and someone in pit shouted, "Ay, put ah breast in dat chile mout!"

Another time, during a Chinese 'Wang Yu' movie, a real fight broke out between two 'bad johns'. I didn't know whether to look at the fight on the screen or the one taking place in front of me. These sword fight movies were very popular at the time, even though they became more contrived. There was the 'One-Armed Master', the 'Drunken Master', the 'Blind One-Armed Master', and so on. People just loved it. An Asian flu once hit Trinidad and it was dubbed the 'Wang Yu'.

Chapter 33

It was Robbie who organized the morocoy races in class, 'morocoy' being the local word for tortoise. While playing cricket in the savannah during our lunch break, the ball went down into the drain. He crawled under the pavement, but instead of the ball he found two of the reptiles. They became out 'race horses', with big money being bet on them.

We'd label them '1' and '2' with chalk, and set them walking forward along the aisle between the rows of desks. Near the top, Robbie would quickly turn them around when the teacher wasn't looking. The one who reached back first was the winner. A lot of lunch money was won and lost on the outcome. Sometimes there'd be a photo finish leading to silent squabbles. One day our Maths teacher, who we called 'Cheesy' because he was red, caught Robbie in the act of turning them around. He told him to leave his relatives at home.

Our geography teacher was old Mr. Goddard, a tall devout man who ran the 'Youth for Christ' club in school. For some reason, before each of our classes, he'd kneel down and ask for the Lord's help. He was a gifted illustrator and once spent half a period drawing a detailed map of South America, shading the relief regions in various colors. He also put Robbie out of the class, which was his standard procedure.

Standing outside, Robbie noticed the principal coming up the stairs with a whip in his hand. That didn't bode well. He had to think fast. The only valid reason for being outside a class was if the teacher asked you to clean the duster. As such, he ran into the room while Mr. Goddard's back was turned, and quickly erased the map. He then went back out and pretended to be cleaning the duster as the principal passed. Mr. Goddard was just about to begin the class when he turned around and saw the map missing, with Robbie outside blowing on the duster. He knelt down and began praying again

I once asked Robbie about his ambition in life. He said he wanted to be a professional sky-larker. He just needed someone to pay him to sky-lark. Many years later, when I was stressed out flying the DC-9 into high-density areas, I decided to do a course in transcendental meditation.

'TM' was popular at the time due to the Beatles' involvement with Maharishi Yogi. Who should turn out to be my instructor but Robbie himself. He gave me a quick lesson and charged me $700, proving that he'd achieved his goal. I never bothered to meditate since I didn't like the stupid mantra he gave me.

I also attended a seminar on meditation given by a visiting swami from India. He spoke of awareness, stress relief, self-development and a higher state of consciousness. A few days later on a flight to Tobago I saw him disembark, followed soon after by a young girl who was in the class. I don't know who they thought they were fooling. Poor guy - I guess he needed some stress relief.

Chapter 34

The few qualified teachers were reserved for the 'A' stream 'bright boys'. The only thing I was any good at, besides English, which I spoke fluently, was woodwork. I'd get 98% for my ashtrays and toothbrush holders, and was glad to help the other guys who were hopeless with tools. I'd depend on that mark to bring my overall average above 45% which was a bare pass.

Throughout my life I've only done well at things which are of practical value. As such I was particularly bad at Geometry and Latin. I didn't see how a triangle touching the sides of a circle would change my life in any meaningful way. As for Latin, it was a dead language which should have been cremated a long time ago. I used to get negative percentages since one mark was subtracted for every error made.

Our Latin teacher, Scofield Pilgrim, was an avid cricket fan. Before the class, someone would raise a controversial point, such as Roy Fredericks being a better opener than Conrad Hunte. That would set him off on a tangent. We'd then sit back and relax while he'd vigorously dispute the claim, all thoughts of Latin mercifully forgotten.

Scofield was also a pianist and leader of the QRC Jazz band. I'd taught myself to play the trumpet and became the front man of that venerable institution. I replaced another student, Milton, who smoked weed and would play off key when high. While on stage Sco would point at you and you'd have to start improvising. It was a magical time for me, jamming with guys who would go on to become professional musicians.

There's no closer bond than members of a band. Each was respected for his talent and virtuosity. We were invited to play at various school events around the country. I had use of my mother's old Hillman, and we'd squeeze the whole group into it, including drums, amplifier, double bass and tenor pan. The guys had to lie on the floor, but we enjoyed every minute.

I once played guitar for the St. Joseph's choir at the Schools' Music

Festival. During rehearsals I developed a crush on their lovely guitarist, Nancy. While on stage at Queen's Hall we were chatting happily and forgot why we were there. A nasty look from the choir mistress clued us in. Sadly, I never saw Nancy again. I always thought that no girl would be interested in me, so never 'tried a ting'. Not being 'buff proof' I was afraid of rejection.

Our drummer was a brilliant quiet guy named Ronnie. We had the greatest respect for him. After college, he went to the States and got his Masters' degree in music. One day, while teaching a class, some police officers came in and arrested him. He was handcuffed and hustled out before his stupefied students. Turned out that, unknown to him, a set of drums which he'd bought from someone was stolen property. Many years later, when he was back in Trinidad, I got in touch with him. I wanted to try and get the band back together, but he wasn't interested. He'd sworn never to touch a drum again.

Chapter 35

Khalid jamming with calypsonian 'Crazy' in my studio

Sofi recording one of her many compositions.

*Shaheeba's watercolor painting of me
ketching my rass on the saxophone*

All my children are talented musicians. Mickhaiel was a violinist with the St. Joseph Chamber Orchestra, while Sofi was twice named best guitarist at the National Schools' Parang Competition. Khalid is also a guitarist and composes digital music for film clips, along with his international musical associates.

We still get together occasionally to have jam sessions. Shaheeba plays the flute and I'd join in on acoustic guitar, harmonica or keyboards. At the age of 70 I'm now teaching myself to read music on the saxophone, probably the most difficult thing I've ever done, and that includes special relativity, string theory and quantum mechanics.

After the kids grew up and left the nest I wanted to keep in touch with the music. I did a course in sound engineering at the Caribbean Sound Basin and set up a home studio. My hope was to record the old calypsonians who were dying out like flies.

I put an ad in the newspapers, but the only ones to respond were hip-hop artists. This was not what I had in mind. Just the same I was very impressed with these 'homies'. They were as good as any of the famous rappers in the States.

Normally I'd charge $100 to record a demo, but one group of rastas couldn't afford it. I'd not only tape them for free but had to drop them home afterwards since they had no money for bus fare. They were extremely polite, and after each session would ask "So what you think, uncle?" I'd honestly say, "You guys are the best." I still listen to their tracks with delight.

One peculiar character was a guy named Chuck. Unlike the other stragglers, he was clean cut and well dressed. He was very interested in my coin collection, especially those from African nations. He said he was in the special forces and had been deployed in that region. All his songs had a military slant, like 'All Troops United'.

Months later I found out that he was the son of ex Liberian President Charles Taylor, who was serving a 50-year sentence for terrorism, murder, rape and using child soldiers. Chuck was his army chief, and was wanted for war crimes in Sierra Leone. He had relatives in Trinidad and was hiding out here. After recording his album he flew to the States and was promptly arrested.

Chapter 36

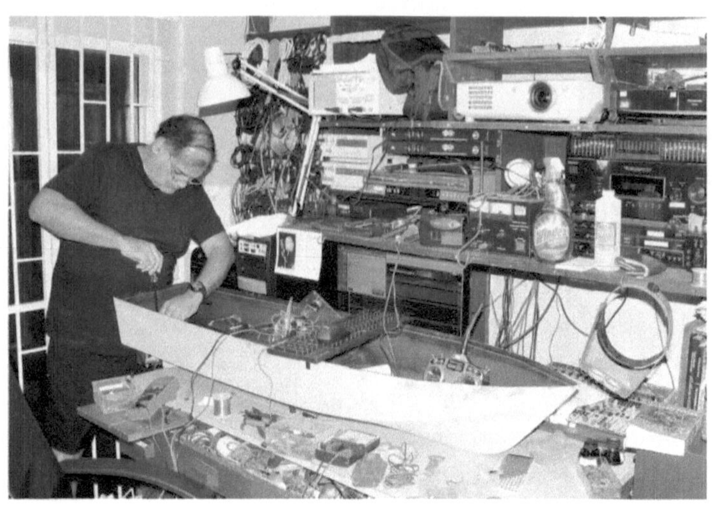

Fast Patrol Boat model

During the summer holidays I had the keys to the QRC workshop and spent my days building radio-controlled model boats. The carpentry skills I developed came in handy when I had to refurbish a real yacht.

My interest in anything else was zero. Needless to say, when O-level results came out I failed everything except English and Literature (woodwork, unfortunately, wasn't part of the exam). It was the lowest point of my life. Out of school at age 15, my disgusted father offered to get me a pushcart to sell shave ice in the street. Even my dog turned up his nose.

Based on my distinction in English and my young age I was offered a repeat. The principal, going through a list, mumbled "Lemee see...there's room in 5B, 5C, 5D..." I said, "There's room in 5A". He looked up in surprise and said, "You want to go in 5A?" I knew if I was back in 'B' stream the result would be no different. I was overjoyed when he said, "OK, I'll put you there."

The 5A guys had done an accelerated course and had already sat the exam in 4th form. They were the cream of the crop. They regarded my presence with some disdain. After my depressing experience, I was determined never to fail again. With proper teachers for a change, I excelled and placed second in our first exam. After that, Gerry was the man to watch.

I passed all subjects with good grades which allowed me to enter 6th form. My father was so pleased he scratched a notch on the doorpost of his office. That meant he expected me to take over his radiology practice one day. No pressure. However, that was not to be.

Chapter 37

A-levels was an exhilarating experience. The teachers treated you like an adult and expected you to work on your own. My first day in Chemistry however came as a shock. Our teacher, a much-revered Mr. Norman Lambert, told us to forget everything we'd been taught about atoms in the past. Instead, he spoke of 4sp3 hybrid electron orbitals, and derived their wave function equations. Thoroughly lost, I whispered to my friend Rishi, "What am I doing here?" He replied, "Is not wha you doing here. Is wha he talkin' bout!" I remained confused for the next two years, especially in Physics. Not having done add maths or A-level maths, calculus for me was totally incomprehensible.

On the bright side, lower 6th was an opportunity to take it easy and get involved in school activities. In those days you sat the exam at the end of the second year, so there was no pressure in the first. I was surprised to be made a prefect since I was not one of the 'bright boys'. It was probably due to my extracurricular activities since they preferred well-rounded students.

In the early days, prefects were feared and respected. They wore ties and clip-on shades. Friday afternoon was the prefect's detention. Unlike the teacher's detention, which was one hour long, there was no time limit on theirs. Parents would sometimes wait till dark to collect their delinquent offspring. They were supported by the Lal, and were a law unto themselves.

With the new wishy-washy administrations, prefects lost their authority. I once caught a boy smoking behind the cafeteria and took him to the principal. This was a serious offense, punishable with suspension. I was therefore surprised when, sometime later, I saw him running around, jeering and pointing at my out-of-style 'gun mouth' pants. I went to the principal and asked him what he did to the boy. He said, "I put him to stand outside my office for 10 minutes and inconvenienced him!" What??? As prefects we were not allowed to hit anyone. When confronted with disrespectful individuals, we'd take off our ties, give them a clout and put our ties back on.

Chapter 38

Nalini

The first thing I did on turning seventeen was sign up for driving lessons. My instructor was a guy named Neville. He was the only one who didn't have dual controls, which gave him ulcers. He used to curse in the worse possible way, and I learned a lot about my family from him. The day before my exam he threw me out the car in the middle of nowhere. As he drove off he said, "Doh worry, you go pass. All allya shitongs does pass."

Many people are so nervous in the exam that their feet shake on the clutch. If you stall the car twice that's a fail, and many students don't make it out of the Licensing Office compound. Accustomed to being abused, I was pleasantly surprised when my examiner was actually polite. The driving test was a breeze. I began to see why Neville had a 100% success rate. These days most people just pay a bribe, which is what I did for my motorcycle license. It cuts a long story short.

Having my license meant I could use my Mom's car to go to school instead of having to ride. One day I saw a girl standing at the corner of La Horquette Road waiting for a taxi. She was slim and had long black hair which came down to her waist. Up until then I had no interest in girls – I was more into boats and planes. That changed instantly.

I offered her a lift and she accepted. Her name was Nalini and she lived way down south. She was doing a course in computers and was staying with a family who lived up the road. Each day I'd time my movements to try and meet her. Eventually we made it official and I gave her a lift every day.

They say your first love is always special, and this was certainly so. Unfortunately, after a few months, she was accepted as a flight attendant with LIAT (Leeward Islands Air Transport), and had to move to Antigua. Long distance relationships are difficult and don't always work. Eventually, my sister Daphne, who worked for the airline, told me it was best to forget about her. I would later find out why.

Chapter 39

In 6th Form, I met some guys who were to remain my best friends for life. First, there was Terry, the son of a wealthy dentist, Dr. Kendal Lee. As such, he was privileged and moved in elevated circles. He once said he had two types of friends – high-class friends and friends like us. We never let him forget that remark. He and I were very close because we were both into electronics, gadgets and photography. While not a scholarship winner like his two brothers who went to CIC, by liming with us he grew up normal. Okay, there was the time he set off a smoke bomb and the school had to be evacuated, but that was an accident.

We were inseparable and often got into weird situations. Once while driving through a residential area we saw a sign advertising a 'Magnetic Energy Enhancer'. Intrigued, we decided to check it out. We met an old man in his garage who said that when placed around the penis, the copper ring improved concentration and mental acuity. I wondered how a copper ring could be magnetic, and asked him what about women? He said they wore it on their wrist, but it was more effective when placed around a penis. He said he'd have to do a fitting on us to get the correct size. He went in the back and came out with a dirty piece of string. That's when we decided we'd seen enough. We hurried out of there laughing our heads off.

To this day I remain skeptical of all forms of 'holistic' remedies. Too often I hear of people trying to treat their conditions on the internet. 'Cures' for cancer could be anything from herbs to coffee enemas. By the time they get around to seeing an oncologist it's often too late.

Terry and I went everywhere with our cameras. That gained us access to private functions since people thought we were from the press. If, while driving through the countryside, we came across an Indian wedding, we'd just stroll in and be treated like honored guests. That took care of food and entertainment for the evening. One of my wedding pictures actually appeared in the papers, to my surprise. The professional photographers tended to resent my presence since the hosts often used my free photos instead of paying for theirs.

The first time I ate at a Hindu wedding the food was placed in front of me on a large fig leaf. This consisted of dhal, rice, and a sappy assortment of pureed vegetables. I waited for a knife and fork but realized that everyone was eating with their hands. I don't mind eating roti with my hands, but this runny mess was something else. I was only half Indian and was feeling awkward. I wondered how Terry, being Chinese, was making out. I looked across and saw him happily scooping up the food and stuffing it in his mouth.

At another wedding, the proud father of the bride insisted I go into his daughter's bedroom where intricate hanna designs were being drawn on her hands. I tried my best but couldn't get the pretty young girl to smile. I soon realized why. It was an arranged marriage, and the groom was a drunken old slob who she'd only met the week before. He looked like he'd beat her if her sada roti wasn't round or didn't swell. She would have to live with him and his witchy mother in a board house in Monkey Trace, Barrackpore, far removed from her comfortable home in Lange Park.

Hindu fathers were quick to marry off their daughters who were considered a useless burden. They would often have to pay a large dowry to get them off their hands. These girls would be treated like slaves, and would only gain some standing when they had a 'boy chile'. I found it strange that they would go on to treat their own daughter-in-law the same way one day.

In Trinidad, instances of child brides are among the highest in the Caribbean. Muslims could marry as young as 12 and Hindus at 14. Orisas could marry once they reached 16, while Christians had no age restriction at all. Dating back for centuries, Indian, Muslim and other marriages were not recognized by the state, only Christian marriages were considered legal. Faced with this reality, the Hindu Women's Organization (HWO) consulted with other Hindu, Muslim, Orisa and Christian leaders and went into action. Once the government took notice, it began holding its own forums and debates. The public also started paying attention after the passing of the Children's Act, which raised the issue of child marriage in the country. After years of mobilization, the outdated marriage laws have finally been abolished.

My camera was on an old 'Rollie' which my Dad handed down to me. It was completely manual, and even required a separate light meter to determine the exposure. It took 5 minutes and a lot of preparation to set up a shot, which probably explains why my best photos were taken with it. My Dad taught me the art of composition, and how to develop film and print color photos and slides. Later, after seeing a candid portrait I did of my sister Karen at a wedding, he began referring to me as 'the master.' Coming from him that was high praise indeed.

Terry meanwhile had a professional automatic Nikon F1, with an 80- 200mm zoom lens and motor drive. That came in handy many years later when we found ourselves on a nudist beach on the French Riviera. Some topless young mademoiselles were playing beach volleyball right in front of us. Terry was mesmerized. He ran through a roll of 36 film in less than a minute, overheating his motor drive and himself. Once, when he was about to board the BOAC VC10 flight back to the UK where he studied, he realized he'd left his camera at home. His father called out "Get a new one in Duty Free! And get one for your brother!"

If I spent a night by him I'd have to sleep on the floor because his king- sized 4 poster bed was his workbench. His long-suffering mother, Ave, was very serene and tolerant. Nothing fazed her. One morning she came into his room, stepped over me and just said, "Hi Gerry". When she asked Terry what he wanted for breakfast he said a beer, which she brought for him on a tray. Seeing my surprise she explained that Terry was different from other people.

Terry was a valued member of the group because he had a small jeep called a mini-moke. He also had access to his father's classic Mercedes Benz and brand-new Toyota Corolla. We'd all pile into one of these cars and go roaming around the country for days on end. On one such excursion we found a dark quiet place to camp for the night. Sometime later we realized it was a cemetery. We packed up our stuff and relocated. On another occasion it rained heavily and the road was flooded. A doubles man was stranded and asked if we could give him a drop. He sat in the back with his box on his lap, and made free doubles for us all the way home.

Another trip didn't end so well. We forgot to put coolant in the

Corolla's radiator, and it overheated. We filled it with red Solo, the only liquid we had, which promptly cracked the engine block. We told Terry's father and he instructed his driver to get a new engine.

These walkabout trips were entirely random. I'd be awakened late at night by the guys at the window saying, "Gerry, yuh wasting time!" That meant I'd have to get in the jeep where I'd fall back to sleep, not knowing where we were going or when I'd be back.

Once, when I was living with my father, he didn't see me for 3 days. He called my mother to find out if she knew where I was. She asked him if his car was in the garage. He said yes. She said, "Then what you're worried about?" She was more concerned about her car than me.

There was one time when Terry got me in trouble. He'd developed a crush on Shirley, the daughter of a man who owned the roti shop we patronized. The father was very strict and didn't allow his daughters go out. This frustrated Terry. One day he gave me a note to give her. When I went to the shop I didn't see her so I gave the envelope to her father.

The next day I went to buy my roti and the father glared at me while the sisters giggled in the back. When she got a chance Shirley showed me the note which read, "Leave your window open. I'm coming with a ladder tonight." It was signed, "Terry," except that the 'T' looked like a 'G'. Fifty years later Shirley and I still laugh at that incident.

Chapter 40

Terry's father was a chef, an artist and a musician. He co-authored a book on Caribbean cooking with Errol Barrow, the Barbadian Prime Minister. He once invited me to spend a weekend with his artsy friends at Gasparee Island. I had a boat and they needed transport. I got a chance to watch great painters like Boscoe Holder and Noel Vaucrosson at work. That sparked my interest in painting since they made it look so easy. I decided to specialize in portraiture using watercolor pencils and acrylics, but it was many years before I was any good. I prefer to paint pretty girls since that increases the chances of a beautiful portrait. I never sell my paintings, but frame and give them to the models. I tell them it will be worth something when I'm dead, but don't get any funny ideas.

Shaheeba, who tends to outdo me in my hobbies, is fast becoming an accomplished artist. She collaborates with Jackie Hinkson, Trinidad's premier watercolorist. She did this one of our Prime Minister, Dr. Keith Rowley, when he toured the construction site of the hospital's new Central Block, and gave it to him. As Hospital Medical Director she has been involved in all phases of its design and construction, She hopes it will be completed before she retires since it will need to be staffed and equipped. Everyone knows she's the best man for the job.

While on Gasparee, Boscoe did a quick monochrome painting of me, which was amazing. He captured my likeness with just a few deft strokes of his brush. As much as I wanted, I didn't dare ask him for it. Many years later, when I thought I could afford it, I visited him at his home in Woodbrook. He remembered me because I'd warned him against swimming between the boat and the jetty, a dangerous thing to do. He looked for the painting but gave up, saying it had probably been destroyed in a fire at his studio. While we chatted, he took out a pencil and did a sketch of me. It hangs at a place of honor in my home.

<h1 style="text-align:center">Chapter 41</h1>

My next 'brudder' was Oswin, who was from Bethel Village in Tobago. He was tall and handsome, and I was honored to be included in his close circle of friends. He spoke with a Tobagonian accent and would say things like "Shit is shit, but damn shit eh no shit" - words of wisdom which I often quote. When annoyed he'd describe someone as being a 'bottom scratch' or an 'ant's bamsee'. Don't ask me to explain. On parting he'd say, "Walk on de side" or "Tell tanty hello." None of us had a tanty.

He was a regular on our boat trips to collect marine specimens for our saltwater aquarium. We'd free dive and catch fish hiding under rocks, using a mosquito net. My dad's old 16 HP Westbend outboard motor was unreliable and often gave trouble to start. During one such occasion Ozzie wanted to put the throttle on full and start the engine in gear. I warned him if we did that someone would fall off the boat. He did it anyway and yours truly went flying. The boat shot off with a bunch of guys who didn't know how to drive. I waved my hands to attract their attention in case they didn't realize I was missing. They eventually did and turned around. The boat was now coming towards me at full speed, and I had to dive to avoid being run over.

During the holidays some of us spent a few days with his family in Tobago. His mother was pleased that he had Indian pals who were so close. We were surprised since we never considered our racial differences. While there, he introduced us to pacro tea, a local aphrodisiac. It's made by boiling an intertidal mollusk that clings tightly to the rocks, and drinking the water.

Many years later on a flight to Tobago, my co-pilot Jake, complained that he was having difficulty keeping up with his second wife who was young and steamy. He said that, after a few rounds, he'd be shooting dust. I told him about the pacro tea. When we landed, he spoke to the station manager and asked her to get him some. On a subsequent flight he told her the pacro wasn't hacking it - he needed something stronger. She said there was a fish head which was supposed to work better. He told her, "Gimme de whole fish!"

Like all my friends, Ozzie was brilliant, and got his degree in transport engineering. He went on to head the Trinidad and Tobago Airport Authority. He recently retired after many years managing private airports in the States.

Chapter 42

Next was Trevor, who I knew from primary school. His parents were teachers, and he was the brightest of the bunch. He used to drive his father's Renault crazily without a license. When he did go for his driving test, I was surprised to hear he'd failed. I asked him what happened. He said, "That examiner didn't like my head. He was out for me. He failed me just because I went up a one-way street." Knowing Trevor, he probably did so at 60 miles an hour. His girlfriend's father didn't like him, so he asked our Chemistry teacher, Mr. Lambert, to write him a recommendation. It probably said, "Dear Mr. Tam. Trevor is basically a decent young man, even though he hangs out with a bunch of good-for-nothings."

Trevor and I play guitar and share a love for music. He's now an accomplished opera singer and gave an amazing recital at his church recently. He was the best man at my wedding and the truest friend one could ask for.

Colin was also a valued member of our posse since he got his grandmother to catch frogs for our zoology dissections. He once invited us to spend the night at his house, which he said was haunted. The legend, if I remember, was that the previous owner had killed his wife by running her over with his car. It was thought her restless spirit was occupying the front room. Colin's father, a mathematics lecturer, had actually been thrown off the bed while sleeping there.

The room was boarded up, but we were determined to spend the night. Armed to the teeth with cutlasses, kitchen knives and sticks we were ready to take on any spirit, real or imaginary. While waiting for Ozzie, we started telling ghost stories. By the time he was ready we had gotten so spooked we called off the trip. Colin and I would go on to live in Jamaica, trying to get into medicine.

The one misfit in our group was Kenrick. Unlike my other friends who were active sportsmen, Kenrick was short and pudgy. His father was a schoolmaster who owned a Hindu school. He forced Kenrick to 'beat book' (study) at an early, which affected his eyes. He had to wear thick glasses to see anything. While not one of the 'bright boys', he had a photographic memory which got him through O-Levels. If you asked him a question in zoology, he'd quote the page number and recite the information from the text book that had 600 pages.

He was addicted to spaghetti westerns which were popular at the time. He called himself Sanchez and 'smoked' his pencil as if it was a cigar. His eyes would also flutter if he saw a pretty girl, like his hero, the rugged actor Klaus Kinski.

He was resilient and knew no shame. On Sports Day he entered all events, including the 400m hurdles. Unable to jump over the bars, he knocked down each one. He'd then stop to put it back in place before proceeding to the next. Medals were being awarded for the next race while Kenrick was still coming round the bend.

One Sunday he went to the Holy Faith Convent bazaar in Couva. There he saw a girl named Christine who blew his mind. He wanted to meet her but didn't know how. Colin had a cousin who went to that school. We told Kenrick that, if he wrote the girl a note, the cousin would deliver it to her. He didn't know what to say, so we wrote a love letter for him. In it, we said he'd like to meet her at the Couva Junction on Sunday. We also coached him on how to act near a girl. No pencil smoking, no eyes fluttering.

Surprisingly she showed up, probably not knowing who he was or what he looked like. They spent the evening together in her father's grocery below the house. The next day we were all anxious to hear how things went. He said, "It was great! All the tuna fish you could eat!"

They continued dating which was strange since Christine was an attractive, sophisticated girl. He was my lab partner at UWI (The University of the West Indies), but I never saw him. Any chance to sneak out was spent with her. The next day he would turn up and demand, "Barrow! Results!" Fifty years later they are happily married with two daughters. I still don't know what she sees in him.

Chapter 43

Sandrah

My mother treated my schoolmates as her own. She would make her tasty sweet-bread whenever we had a fete match. Years later, Ozzie would call her frequently from the States, which made her day. I was very grateful to him for that. He called me to express his condolences on her passing, just as I got the news myself.

We'd meet at Tranquility each night, supposedly to study, but it was more of a support group. A-level Physics and girlfriend issues were a toxic combination. We all had 'tabanka', except Ozzie. He had a golden gift of gab and did not 'tote' on any woman.

One night, while we were 'studying', Ozzie introduced me to a girl named Sandrah who was doing an evening course there. Her brother was blind, and she was learning to read braille. She was a born-again Christian, and a welcome change from my first girlfriend who was deceitful, to put it mildly.

She lived on Clifton Hill, Laventille. Anything east of the Dry River, 'behind the bridge,' was gangster territory. Her house was at the very top, up a long flight of steps. One night, as I was walking up the winding road to visit her, I saw three 'brothers' sitting on a culvert. I know trouble when I see it.

Surely enough, as I got closer, one of them got up and started walking towards me. As he came close, I looked him in the eye and slowly reached into my back pocket. He stopped abruptly and allowed me to pass. I then took out my kerchief and mopped my sweaty brow.

On Fridays I would go with Sandy and her many sisters to their small evangelical church in New Town. The young people were friendly, and I enjoyed singing the songs. I was beginning to think this religion thing might not be so bad after all. Maybe I should give it a shot.

One night the pastor had an alter call. That's where all those who were prepared to devote their life to Christ had to raise their hands and come forward. Even though I'd been thinking about it I hadn't reached that level of commitment. I still liked my wayward ways and material stuff. I didn't want to deceive the pastor in case there was a special place in hell for people who did that. As such I remained seated, which was very obvious, to say the least.

The next Friday, when I went to pick up Sandrah, there was a prayer circle in progress. They were praying for my everlasting soul. Each one tried to outdo the other in condemning me, threatening me with fire and brimstone. The pastor told Sandy that a Christian girl could not be dating a sinner. She had to choose between me and Jesus. I said that was unfair - I tried walking on water once and nearly drowned. She had to end our relationship, but we remain dear friends to this day.

Chapter 44

Shaheeba

We all married our high school sweethearts. One day I got home from school and there was a TV show in progress called College Quiz. QRC was up against St. Augustine Girl's High School. I stopped to watch and noticed a very pretty girl on the SAGHS team. Next day in school I asked the guys if they saw the show. Colin said, "Did you see that girl?" Seems they all did. We needed to find out more about her, so we consulted Neil, the QRC Head Boy. Neil was the eldest and wisest, and a Godfather to us all. He coached women's hockey and had extensive contacts throughout the girls' schools. Within hours he had all the information we needed, including her name, number, address and father's occupation.

We couldn't all check her out, so we decided to raffle her. I wrote her name on a piece of paper and put it in a geometry tin, along with other blank pieces. I rigged the contest by writing her name the biggest piece of paper, which was easy to find. I won and gave her a call. My sister, who loved a bacchanal, shouted, "Mummie, Gerry's talking to the girl on TV!"

She invited me to a Christmas concert at UWI and we became fast friends. While she was very pleasant and talented, I became more interested in her best friend, Shaheeba. There's girlfriend material and there's wife material. Fortunately I had the sense to know the difference. Five years later, when I informed her father that we were getting married, he said that Shaheeba was special. I said I knew - that's why I was marrying her.

Chapter 45

The Advanced Level GCE exams were difficult. The first thing I'd do when opening a paper is browse through the questions. I'd put a tick on the ones I could do and a cross on the ones I couldn't. It didn't auger well when most of the questions had double crosses. One of the Physics questions was a repeat from a past paper I'd done before. I knew the answer but couldn't remember the method. I had to do some reverse engineering. It was going to be rough.

While waiting for results, I spent the summer doing voluntary work on a Cree native reserve in Northern Ontario. Ozzie had put me on to an organization called Frontiers Foundation in Canada. They did projects in various parts of the world. He had gone on one the year before, and Sandy and I were keen to take part. The Foundation paid our airfare to Canada and for our meals and accommodation.

Students from all over the world were housed in a church building in Toronto for a few days before setting off to their various destinations. It was most wonderful meeting all these young enthusiastic people. The fact that we could help ourselves to unlimited food in the kitchen was a great plus. Sandy's uncle, who lived in Toronto, took us for lunch at a smorgasbord. I don't know these things still exist, but for $10 you could eat all you want. Despite his long skinny frame Ozzie went to town, polishing off three heaping plates of food. I suspect they raised the price after that.

My group consisted of four Canadians, plus Lilori from Tobago, and an elderly guy named Kalua from Sri Lanka. Our group leader, Kyle, was a tall lanky Australian. We boarded a Boeing 727 and flew north to the town of Timmins. The residents there like to say it's the largest city in the world. That's because the sparse wooden cabins were spread over an area larger than Tokyo.

We then got on a rickety old DC-3 which was held together by duct tape. We landed a few hours later on a gravel strip in the middle of nowhere. After waiting around on our own for several hours a native arrived in a canoe to take us to the village. While driving on the wide muddy river

I took out a mint and flipped the wrapper over the side. I got a stern lecture about polluting the environment from Janet, an unattractive disagreeable girl. I told her it was just a tiny wrapper, but she said that one day I'd become a major industrialist and do the same thing. Whatever.

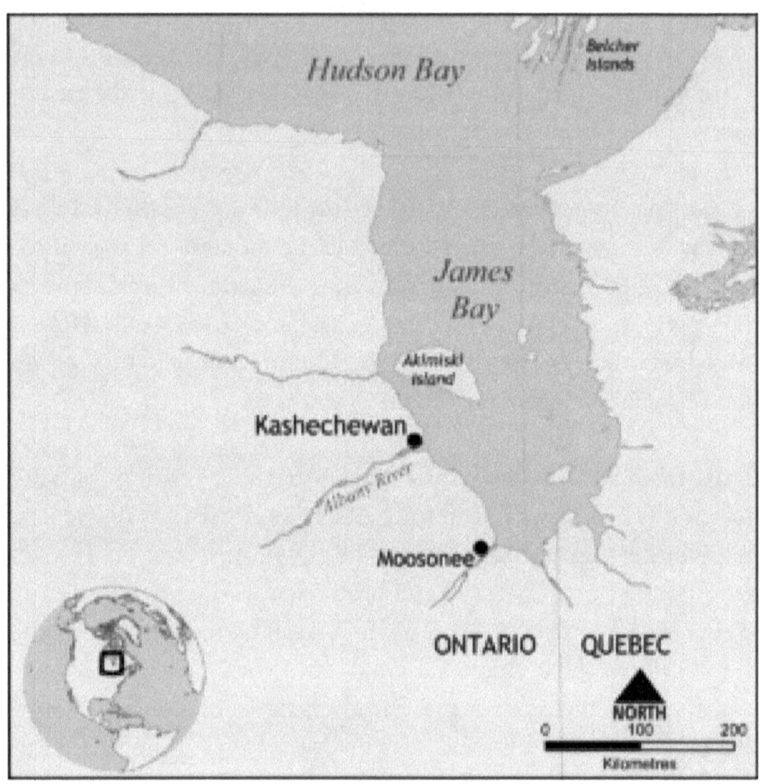

Chapter 46

The village of Kashechewan is situated on the western coast of James Bay in Northern Ontario. It contained about 20 wooden houses, located on the banks of the Albany River. It was completely isolated, the nearest town being Moosonee, 100 miles away. Our job was to repair houses damaged by a spring flood a few months earlier. We also had to rebuild one that belonged to a guy who got drunk and attacked his house with a chainsaw. I was a bit disappointed since I thought we'd be building houses from scratch, as Ozzie did on his project. Being an engineering student, he re-designed their roof to provide better heat dissipation. I was also displeased that we'd be staying in the modern apartment used by the Canadian teachers who were home on vacation. I had visions of living in a teepee.

Each day six of us would take our tools and go to work while the remaining two would stay back and cook. That worked well until two Canadians ended up on KP. We came home, tired and hungry, to find two pots of soup on the table. One was a cloudy pink while the other was brown and smelled like fermented horse pee. We asked about the pink one and they said it was canned tomato soup with powdered milk. Without asking about the other, Lilori gave a loud 'steups', went into the kitchen and started stewing some chicken. Like most West Indians, male or female, she was an excellent cook. We made sure the kitchen roster never paired two Canadians again.

All food had to be flown in by seaplane, and was expensive. When it was my turn to cook, I went to the village grocery and bought a leg of lamb. I roasted it, along with baked potatoes smothered with sour cream, a cheesy macaroni pie and buttered corn on the cob. My step-mother Rita was an excellent cook and I'd picked up a thing or two. Everyone thought the meal was fabulous, but Kyle was livid. He saw the grocery bill and thought I'd spent too much. He said the money to fund these projects came from the 'March of Dimes', little children trudging in the snow to beg for pennies. I felt guilty after that. I felt even worse when he imposed strict rations. We'd have to bake our own bread and he'd sleep by the refrigerator to make sure no one sneaked in for a midnight snack.

The Foundation was worried about us when they saw our food bill. They thought we were eating tree bark. They sent Steve, a young amiable official, to check on us. He made a huge meal of lamb chops, mashed potatoes and beans.

We actually had leftovers! That didn't last long. As soon as he left, we were back on our starvation diet.

Being an Aussie he swore at everything in the most vulgar way. By now he and plump, pock-faced Bobbie were having an affair, which was against company policy. That had us pissed since she acted like royalty. Things got more unpleasant as the weeks wore on. The following year I was chosen to be a group leader and was determined that things on my project would be different.

Chapter 47

The Cree Indians, led by Chief Silas, were very friendly people. They spoke halting English, but we were able to communicate fairly well. The girls were very attractive and were fascinated by my brown skin. They had never seen a colored guy before, so I was a novelty. At night they'd come outside my door, calling my name. They wanted me to join them in a shed at the back which was used by the telecommunications technicians. I was engaged at the time and was able to resist the temptation.

One night two older women came calling on me. One of them, who spoke English, told me that the other wanted to invite me to a dance in the village. In the dark I recognized Claris, a married woman. "What about her husband?" I enquired. "That okay," she said. "He out hunting." I could just imagine Sitting Bull, returning with a grizzly bear over one shoulder and shotgun in hand, seeing me dancing with his wife. I respectfully declined.

These women earned money making leather shoes, jackets and beaded necklaces. We all ordered moccasins made from synthetic materials. Janet however, insisted on real leather. She told them to trap a beaver and use its hide. What a hypocrite, I thought. She was the one who lectured me about preserving the environment.

Halfway through the projects, all groups were supposed to go on a one- week retreat. Kyle, who was full swing into his austerity drive, said there'd be no retreat for us. Morale sank even lower. That wasn't the only thing to sink.

Determined to do my own thing, I built a raft out of driftwood logs. I planned to row across the river and live off the land. That day I'd gotten a letter from my fiancé Shaheeba. It was the first time I'd heard from her, since the seaplane delivered mail infrequently. The others, who'd seen her lovely photo, wanted to hear what she had to say. I certainly wasn't going to read it to them. Instead, I put it in my back pocket and boarded my makeshift craft. They all gathered on the bank to bid me farewell.

Halfway across the river the raft became waterlogged and started to sink. I swam back to shore, wet, cold and bitterly disappointed. It was then that my hysterical friends reminded me of the letter in my pocket. I took it out carefully and my worst fears were confirmed. Most of the writing was washed out. That night the hysterics continued unabated as I ironed the letter hoping to recover some precious words.

Chapter 48

Not everything was bad. Chief Silas took us out a couple of times in his canoe. On one fishing trip we were traveling across a wide lake with scattered islands. A young guy named Benjamin from the Mennonite group asked me if I wanted to swim to the island we were passing. I didn't think he was serious, so I said, "After you". Imagine my surprise when the idiot jumped off the canoe. I had no choice but to jump off too.

Big mistake. To begin with, even though it was summer, the water was freezing cold. I got an instant headache. I then realized that this wasn't a lake. I was in a fast-flowing river, too wide to see the banks. We swept past the island and were carried downstream. Silas, who figured we knew what we were doing, drove on, leaving us behind.

Swimming was difficult in the fresh icy water because I had on my coat, sweater and boots. Ben and I soon got separated. Eventually, I managed to make it to one of the islands. Totally exhausted, I did a Robinson Crusoe impression and crawled up on the shore. Just as it was getting dark Silas and the others returned and picked me up. They were more excited about the fish they caught than seeing me alive. It took us a while before we found Ben on another island. He was suffering from hypothermia and was in a bad way.

Sometime later Ben got involved with Elli, Silas's eldest daughter. I asked him if that was wise. He said, "It's no big thing. Old Silas doesn't give a shit." I wasn't too comfortable with that. Native girls used these liaisons to try to get off the reservation, but ended up just being used. There's no doubt that Canadians discriminate against 'first world' people. Bringing home a Cree girl to meet Mum and Dad would not go down well, no matter how pretty she was. Even if Silas didn't mind, the young 'braves' in the tribe certainly did. One day, when Ben was out, they stole into his room and chopped up all his belongings. The Mennonite group was obliged to leave the reservation. I wonder how they explained that to the brethren back home.

Our hunting trip was more successful. We pitched a tent in the marshes and set out with shotguns. There was a gaggle of Canadian geese swimming on the far side of the river. They didn't take us on, knowing they were out of range. Kyle noticed one straggler swimming further up on our side. I crawled behind the levee unseen until he gave me the signal that I'd reached.

I popped up from behind the bank and the bird took off like an F16. I'd never used a gun before but fired in the general direction. At first, nothing happened. The bird then banked sharply to the left and fell in the water. Not having a dog, I had to swim out to retrieve it. Everyone was grateful since we hadn't brought any food. Silas was amazed that I'd actually shot a goose and said it must have been crazy. He carved slabs of rich dark meat from the breast, coated it in flour and fried it. Even without salt or seasoning, it was delicious. Surprisingly, the rest of the carcass was discarded. I wouldn't have minded a thigh and drumstick as well.

I didn't have a change of clothes, and was wet and cold. Silas set up a wood-burning stove in the tent to keep us warm. I put my socks and shoes in the oven to dry them out. Sometime later I opened the door, and the boots came pouring out. The heat had melted the rubber. Silas couldn't contain himself, but I had to go barefoot for the rest of the trip. When we got back, he must have told the villagers. After that, all the children would laugh and call me 'Crazy Goose'. That was my official name from then on.

Towards the end of our stay gold was discovered on the Albany River. After work we'd go panning for gold dust. That was difficult because of the large black flies in the area. They'd land on you and bite off chunks of skin. More annoying were the mosquitoes which were present in the billions. I always thought those were tropical insects but not so, Canada beat us back. They'd be so thick on our window you couldn't see through.

One night one of them managed to get in. Our first impulse was to swat it, but Pam, one of the Canadians, objected. She was a soft-hearted person who didn't believe in killing any living creature. Instead, she cupped it in her hands, opened the window and let it out. The thousands who were liming outside came swarming in. To hell with Pam, we swatted them left and right.

After the fishing trip, Pam saw the dead fish in the kitchen sink. She was apoplectic and locked herself in her room for days. The next time we saw her she was boarding the Twin Otter sea plane and heading back home. She was the first escapee on our project. We all envied her.

It was bittersweet when we too had to go. I got the addresses of the friends I'd made and wrote them next spring when the river thawed. We never did find gold but heard that the Canadian Government was reviewing the treaty to see if the Cree Natives really owned the land. Silas came with us on his way to

Ottawa to argue the case for the indigenous people. I thought, the more things change, the more they remain the same.

While the social aid provided allowed the natives to live comfortably on the reservation there was no industry or employment for the young people. They grew up aimless, drinking moonshine and sniffing glue and gasoline.

Chapter 49

The Band of Brudders

When A - Level results came out I managed to bare-pass all three subjects. I was happy for that because of the struggle involved. I have my pals to thank for seeing me through a very difficult time. 55 years later they remain my closest friends. We call ourselves 'The Band of Brudders' and get together for dinner whenever one comes in from abroad.

We didn't have any fancy graduation ball. Instead we got together with the Bishop's girls and had a party for Mr. Lambert at Trevor's home. The girls didn't have a Chemistry teacher, so he taught at both schools. On Saturday mornings we'd have joint lessons at QRC in the chemistry lab. This gave us a chance to see girls, if not meet them. They sat on stools in the front row while we sat at the back. This gave us a good view as they leaned over.

They kept to themselves, and we thought they were snobbish. Turns out they were more shy than us. In those days few schools were co-ed. Boys and girls were segregated from age six. As such, girls were a mystery to us. We were awkward in their presence and didn't know what to say. Only 'buff proof' Kenrick had the nerve. He passed a note to a pretty one named Indira. The crumpled piece of paper said, "If loving you is wrong, I don't want to be right." She read it, turned around and gave him a nasty look. That didn't faze him. He went on smoking his pencil, eyes fluttering. Indira went on to marry another one of our brudders, Ahmin, thereby keeping her in the family.

At the party we finally got a chance to socialize and get to know them better. I tried dancing but it was hopeless, I was no good at it. If I wasn't stepping on their toes I was going the wrong way. Eventually I got a chance to dance with Diedra, who I had my eye on. Strangely enough it worked out well. Maybe the problem wasn't me. She was very petit and a bit of a tomboy. Her father owned a transport company, and she drove and serviced the trucks. A girl after my own heart.

We presented Mr. Lambert with a lazy boy chair as a token of our appreciation. He was more than just our teacher. He was our confidant who we could go to with any problem. He'd asked me to design the cover of the Chemistry textbook he'd written. When he saw my artwork he smiled and said, "Boy, if push come to shove you will never starve." Puberty was a depressing time for me, so his words of praise lifted my spirits.

After the party Diedra asked me if I could drop her at home. But of course! That would give me a chance to talk to her and get to know her better. Who knows, it might be the start of something. That's when a Chinee guy named Gordon asked if I could drop him home too. I told him to try and get a lift with someone else. I explained that I was trying to get to know this girl, and he'd be cramping my style. He said no one else would take him. He lived further away, which meant I'd have to drop her home first. So that was it, crash and burn before I even got off the ground.

When we got to her home, with all the trucks in the yard, she hesitated before coming out of the car. I didn't even have the manners to open the door for her. By then I'd figured a classy girl like that wouldn't be interested in me anyway, so what's the point. I never saw her again.

Years later, when living in Jamaica, I asked my friend Liz if she knew a girl named Diedra, since they were in the same year. She said, "Of course I knew Diedra. All she ever did was talk about Gerry Barrow." WHATTTT!!!? I wanted to strangle Liz. This was our second year in Jamaica, and she never told me a thing. If I knew that I would have checked her out while home on vacation. Who knows what might have happened?

Not long ago, I dropped by Shirley for a roti. I asked her if she knew a girl named Diedra who lived somewhere nearby. She said, "Yes. In fact she walks past the shop every evening after work. She's a senior nurse, unmarried, and keeps herself well." I asked her where she lived, and she replied suspiciously, "Why yuh want to know?" Knowing us QRC guys since school days, she figured I was up to something. I explained that she was someone I knew a long time ago and just wanted to touch base. She didn't believe that's all I wanted to touch.

Chapter 50

100 year old QRC clock mechanism

Ten years ago the band of brudders had a meeting for our 40th anniversary. We wanted to do something for our beloved school. The historic QRC clock hadn't worked for years. The Principal had gotten an estimate of $270,000 to have it repaired. The guy, who'd fixed the CIC clock, planned to replace the 100-year-old clockwork mechanism with an electric motor. The giant bronze bells, each weighing several tons, would be replaced with loudspeakers playing mp3 chimes from a flash drive.

We thought it would be a shame to condemn this marvelous piece of machinery which had been in place since 1904. The clock was built by Dent's of London, the same company that made Big Ben. I told the guys that, being engineers, they should be able to repair the clock, a purely mechanical device. They twisted that around, saying that, as a pilot, I was accustomed to dealing with 'clocks' in the cockpit. Somehow the responsibility of fixing the thing fell on me.

My first impression was that the clock mechanism was a lot smaller than I expected. Also, it was in fairly good condition for something 100 years old. All the bearings were seized and would have to be freed. It didn't take long to figure out how it worked. The escapement mechanism was similar to one I'd built to control the rudder movement on my model boat.

The clock and bells got their energy from three enormous stacks, weighing about 1000kg each. These were suspended by cables from the top of the tower, 40 feet above. The cables were wound on three separate drums. Cranking up all three weights took a healthy man one hour and two cold Caribs.

Under normal circumstances, the weights would just drop and spin the hands of the clock like a fan. However, the caliper arms of the escapement prevented that from happening, since they jammed against a four-sided flywheel. Each time the pendulum swung it would release one arm of the caliper, allowing the flywheel to move through 90 degrees. The flywheel would then be caught by the other caliper arm and released one second later by the pendulum. This delicate mechanism was responsible for moving the six- foot hands of the clock.

Once I got the clock ticking, the next thing was to adjust the length of the pendulum so its period would be exactly one second. This calibration took several months, using a tiny brass screw at the base. A half-turn either way would result in minutes lost or gained each month. It's such a delicate process that the professional technicians who service Big Ben adjust its period by placing old English coins on the heavy pendulum. That changes its effective length. It would appear that the new decimal currency doesn't work as well.

After much tweaking, I finally got the timing perfect due to a final adjustment by Sheldon, my right-hand man. He'd be up in the tower turning the screw while I observed the clock from outside, communicating by cellphone. It's now accurate to one minute a year, better than the Rolex Micky bought for me. At our group's 50th anniversary last year, we officially handed over the completed project to our grateful alma mater.

Chapter 51

Needless to say, there was no way I was getting into Medicine with three 'E's. The minimum requirement was two 'A's' and a 'B'. I persuaded my father to send me to Mona, Jamaica, where the Medical Faculty was located. I figured that being on-site would give me a slight advantage. I also needed to leave home and live on my own.

I shared a house off campus with Colin and Liz, the sister of another QRC friend. Even though she was our age, she was like a den mother and called us by our surnames. Sadly, she would die a few years later, from what we didn't know. It's possible she was sick all the time but never said anything.

Money was tight and we pooled our limited resources to stretch things out. One bottle of Squeezie had to last the term. I ate beef patties for lunch every day for the next 2 years. The lady would take them out of the oven when she saw me coming.

We had dinner by a woman named Fat Carol who lived up the road. We called her that to distinguish her from two other Carols we knew – Normal Carol and Cockroach Carol, who was small and shriveled. FC had to be the worst cook in the world but needed the money to support her young son Alex. She bought chicken necks wholesale which she alternately stewed and curried. The first time I ate it I nearly choked. On coughing it up I realized the necks still had feathers on them.

Another time she proudly served us pudding for dessert. It was mauve in color and had the consistency of an eraser. Stick your knife in it and not even King Arthur could pull it out. So as not to hurt her feelings we wrapped the dense slabs in napkins and said we'd take it home to eat later. When we got there, we grabbed our landlady's dog, Fluffy, and shoved the pudding down its throat. The poor dog started to cough and gag. After that, he would run and hide whenever he saw us coming. Would you believe she served the same thing the next day? Only this time she froze the batter and called it ice cream.

Our landlady, Miss Simpson, was a sweet soul. She was a single mother, like most Jamaican women we knew, and had a brat for a son. There was a Julie mango tree in her yard, and I picked all the full ones and kept them in my chest of drawers. As they ripened, I'd move them to upper levels, so the top draw had the ripest. Colin told me I really should share them with her, seeing it was her tree. I reluctantly agreed and gave her one. She said, "A mango? For me? Thank you!" That made me feel bad for a while.

One night I came home tired and flopped down on my bed. I was immediately thrown off. Removing the sheet I noticed that the mattress was missing. All I could see were the rusty springs. I asked Miss Simpson about it, and she shyly admitted that she was short on the rent and had to sell the mattress. She was such a lovely person I didn't make a fuss.

The bed was spring-loaded and could fold in two. I'd have to be careful when sleeping since it would often collapse on its own. Eventually I got fed up of being sandwiched between the springs. I got four heavy foundation blocks and tied them to its legs. During the night I'd hear the bed creaking and straining as it tried to get me.

My father had this old-fashioned notion that children studying abroad had to suffer. That's because he lived in England after the war. Money was deposited in my account for modest meals and basic accommodation - nothing more. In my two years in Jamaica I never saw the inside of a car. I either walked or took an overcrowded JOS bus into town. Sometimes there'd be so many people hanging on to the windows that the bus would almost topple over.

For cheap entertainment I'd go to church on Sundays, but by now I was turned off religion. I considered it to be nothing but man-made rituals and dogma, created to enrich and empower those on top. From the televangelists, boasting about their private jets, to the suicide bombers, hoping to enter paradise with its 72 virgins, I was disgusted. In Trinidad we have a well-known pastor who passes around the basket twice saying, "You need to plant a seed if you hope to reap." I'd love to plant a kick up his backside. Another was found with twenty-eight million dollars under his bed. Next Sunday his congregation just added more. Even though there was severe flooding his parish he did nothing to help. Later, as a pilot, I'd fly over Jonestown in Guyana and wonder how people could be so gullible.

Our only extravagance in Jamaica was going to the movies in Half Way Tree, a small town a few miles down the road. The first time I went to the cinema I was shocked to look up and see the moon rising. The auditorium had no roof! One night the police raided the place and collected an enormous pile of guns, ammunition and knives.

On these outings we were joined by Liz's friend, Leslie, a bright and chatty med student. There would always be a debate on what movie to choose. On one occasion the girls wanted to see a comedy called 'Five on the Black Hand Side'. Colin and I were more interested in a soft porn flick called 'The Long Swift Sword of Siegfried'. He and I bought the tickets, and quietly paid for our selection.

The movie started with the Viking, Siegfried, having wild sex with an Amazon woman. Outside, his enemies were approaching on horseback. He slipped out the back while the woman flung open the front door to distract them. Standing stark naked in the doorway, she squeezed her ample breasts, spraying them with milk. Liz and Leslie were appalled, while Colin and I pretended we'd been given the wrong tickets. Leslie is now a consultant nephrologist and member of the Medical Board. She and Shaheeba are close associates. I wonder if she ever believed our lame excuse.

Chapter 52

Colin was an irascible guy who was easily annoyed. He used to curse in his sleep and wake up angry. This was strange since his parents, like all the others, were very pleasant people. His Mom made the best apple pie I ever tasted. We'd come outside their house late at night and sing carols, hoping to get some. Colin's father couldn't understand how come we were caroling in July.

One day, while we were walking through Mona Heights on the way home, he spotted a kaimit tree in someone's yard. I didn't even know what a kaimit was, but he insisted I jump the wall, climb the people's tree and steal their fruit. Hoping they didn't have a dog, I did as instructed, and was soon sending down kaimit for him to catch.

He told me the biggest one was right at the top and insisted I get it. With the sun in my eyes, I reached up and plucked it off the branch. I found it felt soft and squishy. I looked down and realized I was holding a 'jep' nest in my hand. The angry hornets came pouring out, determined to wreak havoc on whoever destroyed their home. Before they could sting me, I let go of everything and came crashing down the tree. I broke branches on the way down and was a bloody mess when I hit the ground. Colin was aghast and said, "Where de kaimit?"

He and I did the same courses and attended classes together. There was a jittery guy named Campbell next to him in the lab who had to be the worst chemist in the world. Each day he'd break several pieces of his Pyrex apparatus, while we tried our best to stifle our giggles. One day he was boiling some acid in a test tube and, instead of putting the flame at the top, he heated it from below. The hot acid came gushing out, burning Colin's hands in the process. He was in bandages for the next few weeks.

On the last day of the year, lockers were inspected to check on our equipment. Anything missing would be deducted from our $50 caution money. We were curious to see Campbell's locker since we figured there'd be nothing left. Miraculously, he had more glassware than when he started! It reminded me of the story of the fishes and the loaves. Years later, when visiting Jamaica, I asked a friend about him. I was told he was teaching chemistry at a government college.

Chapter 53

Jamaica was a violent place, especially around election time. Wearing the wrong color shirt could get you in trouble. The Jamaican Labour Party (JLP), headed by Edward Seaga, was green, while the People's National Party (PNP), led by Michael Manley was orange. Every night you'd hear gunfire as rival groups shot up each other.

One night, while I was returning home from church, I saw three guys standing on the narrow bridge over the aqueduct. Once again, I could sense trouble. Surely enough, as I stepped up to cross, one of them blocked me and pulled out a rachet. That's a switch blade knife which every Jamaican male carries on him. I'd just started karate and had learned a few basic techniques. I stepped sharply into a front stance and put my fist in the guy's face. He said "Oi! Ah karate bwoi!" and stepped aside. As I passed, another grabbed my shoulder. I did a slow back fist strike to his nose, showing how I could break it. He let go and the three of them walked off. They figured I wasn't worth the trouble. I firmly believe that if you show people you are not afraid of them, they will leave you alone.

There was one incident where I was actually robbed. It occurred one night while I was lying on my springs trying to study. I looked across at my window and saw a hand disappearing with my wallet. I tried to grab it, but it was too late. These thieves were known as 'fishermen' because they often came with rods to fish out your valuables.

There were some funny incidents as well, such as the mysterious 'Phantom Phallus'. Late at night, girls of Irvine Hall would see a long penis snaking through their wooden louver windows. A loud scream would indicate that the Phantom had struck again. One night he made the mistake of trying that on a Trini girl. Seeing the lengths of penis coiling on her side table, she emptied her bottle of Matouk's pepper sauce on it. Howls were heard across the campus. That was the last of the Phantom.

There was also the curious case of 'Ralph the Raper'. He would rape several women each night. The Police employed helicopters to search for him. They posted a picture of him in the papers with a wide salacious grin on his face. One night he outdid himself, raping four women in a house. What a vicious brute I thought, until I heard the report from one of the victims. She said, "First he did 'er, then me, then the other two. Then it was my turn again."

It's only when you live abroad that you appreciate home-cooked food. One night on my way home I got a whiff of curry, something I hadn't eaten in months. I turned around and, like a bloodhound, tracked it to its source. A Trini girl was making roti in her room in Irvine Hall, half a mile away. When I got there, I saw a crowd of hungry guys liming outside her door. Unfortunately it was all 'dished up' by then.

Colin and I did try to make roti once, even though my new land lady didn't permit cooking in the room. We kneaded the flour and boiled some split peas to make the filling. We tried to crush it with a bottle, but it didn't work. Just the same we stuffed it in the flour and rolled it with our bottle. We then put it in a pan on our hotplate to fry. The roti tried to rise but the peas acted like an aggregate, keeping it flat. They came out like rock cakes. The curry went a lot better, with both Colin and I trying to remember what our mothers did. He went outside and got some bhaji. It looked like stinging nettle, but I threw it in the pot anyway. The smell of the curry attracted the landlady's dog which started scratching on the door. We had to give him a chicken leg to keep him quiet.

I did get a proper roti once. There was a trade exhibition on Campus, which included food from the various Caribbean countries. At the Guyana booth, there were large hot roti for sale, and I bought one. To make sure I didn't have to share, I hid behind some bushes to eat it. No such luck. Some guys from my Geology class tracked me down and begged me for some. By the time they were finished, there was nothing left for me. The next day they were absent from class. They were all down with acute gastroenteritis even though they had each taken only one bite. Turns out that the roti were made in Guyana the day before and had gone sour. And I was planning to eat the whole thing!

Chapter 54

I was hopeless at sports. I didn't see the point of chasing after a cricket ball in the hot sun. Most likely I'd drop a catch and embarrass myself anyway. Karate was different. It had practical value, and, as such, I excelled. I just wished I'd had the opportunity to learn some sort of self-defense when I was small. It would have prevented all the bullying.

The Mona Karate Club was a serious affair. We trained in the courtyard outside, doing knuckle pushups on hot concrete. We'd then lie on our backs with our legs elevated while the sensei jumped from one stomach to the next. Anyone who let their legs down received a punch in the belly, much to the delight of the others. Most of the time was spent free-sparing. This was meant to be 'no contact' fighting but it didn't always work out that way. Our sensei, Tony Kalloo, had a vicious back kick which he would land on your solar plexus. Being a considerate guy, he'd give you a minute to catch your breath before doing it again.

Within five months I'd gotten my green belt and was selected to represent Mona at the Inter-Campus Games in Trinidad. To get us in shape, Tony took us on a hike up the Blue Mountain. Its peak, at 7,400 ft, is the highest point in Jamaica. We started around 7:00 pm and trudged through the night. The track was steep and rocky, but my Bahamian friend Jeff and I took the lead.

Along the way, we were overtaken by a guy named 'Bigga', no doubt because of his size. I asked him why he had his shoes in his hand, and he said, "Foot could heal". For Jamaicans, dancing shoes are their most prized possessions. An hour later we passed him sprawled out at the side of the track, totally exhausted.

While crossing a river on a log bridge I slipped and fell in the water. As usual I had no towel or change of clothes. Jeff and I were the first to reach the peak and commandeered a tiny wooded shack at the top for ourselves. We were to find out later why it was called the 'ice-box'. Around 2:00 a.m., freezing fog started seeping through the gaps in the walls. I stuffed candy wrappers in the holes, but it did no good. I was wet and freezing. I didn't have a blanket, so decided to 'borrow' Jeff's. I figured he didn't need it since he was already asleep. The next morning he was frozen stiff. I didn't know a black guy could turn blue. It took him hours to thaw out.

I continued training when I came back to Trinidad and got my brown belt. However, while diving off a boat, I struck my shoulder on a rock and tore a ligament. As much as I hate to quit anything, that was it for me. Shaheeba however went on to get her 3rd Dan. My eldest son Mickhaiel also has his black belt, while Khalid got his purple.

Shaheeba, grading for her 3rd degree black belt

Chapter 55

During my first year at University I did Physics, Chemistry and Zoology. I also signed up for Geology which was offered there. This had nothing to do with getting into medicine - it was just something I was interested in. Right now I probably have the most comprehensive mineral collection in the country. Most specimens were collected in the various countries I visited around the world.

Unlike Trinidad, which only has oil, Jamaica is rich in minerals. The field trips into the cockpit country were very interesting. We'd walk along rivers looking for fossils, or crawl into old silver mines to collect galena, the shiny lead sulfide mineral. I carried my diagnostic kit with me, plus a powerful magnet tied with a rope around my neck. Once while walking next to a cliff, the magnet suddenly clamped itself against the rock. Turns out the entire cliff face was made of magnetite, a magnetic form of iron oxide. I was caught by the throat with no one to help me. Fortunately, I was able to reach the knife in my kit and cut myself free.

During a typical class, Dr. Rouble, the huge amiable English mineralogist, would empty a box of rocks on his desk. We'd crowd around excitedly and try to identify them. One of the tests required you to place the specimen at the tip of your tongue and taste it. One guy picked up a crystal of sylvite and slurped his tongue over it. Sylvite is potassium chloride, 13 times stronger than salt. It burned his mouth which he had to flush with water. It was days before he regained his sense of taste.

I was doing Geology as a hobby, and as such I never bought a textbook or took notes. I just looked and listened in fascination. Ironically, I ended up doing better than those who were studying it as a career. I figured if I didn't get into medicine I'd stay on and become a geologist. Our post-graduate demonstrator was doing his thesis on coastal erosion. He spent his weekends on the beach, watching the waves and drinking Red Stripe beer. Unfortunately, during the summer holidays, the wife of one of the English lecturers was raped on campus, and the whole ex-pat staff left. The local replacements didn't inspire me.

Neither Colin nor I wished to remain on campus during the summer vacation. I came up with a scheme which could get us home. I sublet Colin's room to a distant relative named Pat, and put all his stuff in my room. That way we'd just pay one rent. Pat was a final year med student and needed a place to crash. We used the money we saved to buy tickets on the UWI charter flight.

In those days Air Jamaica used to put on an inflight fashion show for the passengers. Their beautiful flight attendants would sashay down the aisle in skimpy swimwear. It was a different scenario when you had a planeload of raucous Trini students going home at 3:00 am. The poor girls would have to dash from one end of the plane to the other while the guys tried to grab them. The theology students were the worst behaved. This was their last fling.

When Colin and I returned to Mona we found our books, clothes and bedding out in the road. It seemed that Pat only stayed a few days. The landlord, who thought whole thing was a scam, threw out all belongings, where it took sun and rain for the next six weeks.

Colin got a room on campus while I went door to door in the rain looking for a place to stay. I eventually found a woman who said she had a room for $40. That was within my budget, so I said I'd take it. The room turned out to be the garden shed with rusty tools stacked in a heap. The shower was a broken PVC pipe sticking out the back wall, with the toilet bowl below. I guess that was for flushing purposes. You had to shit and shower in full view of the neighbors. While the lady was making space by the lawn mower for a mattress I tried to remember if it was Ireland, New Zealand or Jamaica that had no poisonous snakes. I missed my penthouse suite by Narine.

That year I switched subjects, trying my hand at mathematics. What a waste. Never having done add maths or A-level maths, I was at a loss. In the exam the first question was on coordinate geometry, which I knew, but the rest were on integral calculus. I put triple crosses on all of them. I was finished in 5 minutes and tried to hand in my single answer sheet. It was a two-hour exam so I was obliged to sit and wait for 30 minutes before being allowed to leave. When I got home Liz saw me and said, "Barrow, what are you doing here?" I said I could only answer one question. She said, "Are you mad? Get back in the exam!"

Many years later, when visiting Shaheeba in Jamaica, I was walking through campus when the maths professor saw me and shouted,

"You!"

"Who, me?"

"Yes you! We lost your papers! The string must have fallen off and we only got the first page!"

I was tempted to say, "No wonder you bitches failed me," but was afraid he'd ask me to re-sit the exam.

Instead I explained that I'd only done one question. "But you got that right. Why didn't you try the others?"

This poor man had been feeling guilty for years thinking he had failed me unfairly.

Chapter 56

Bugsy with Jessie, our devoted employee of over 30 years

For the third time my grades were not good enough, so I decided to give up on medicine. Colin was brighter than me and he got through. He's now an eminent dermatologist, author, and founder of the Medical Association of Trinidad and Tobago (MATT).

Looking back, maybe it's a good thing I never became a doctor. The sight of blood makes me weak, especially my own. Not long ago I had to do a blood test at the hospital. The young house officer had trouble finding a vessel. He kept jabbing me with a needle while I grew more light-headed. Eventually, I passed out and slid to the floor. They checked my blood pressure which read zero. That meant that I was arresting. My wife was Hospital Medical Director, so everyone was freaking out. They sent for a cardiologist and an ECG machine.

My daughter Sofi, a junior physician, was passing by and noticed the commotion. She came into the room and saw that the sphygmomanometer cuff on my arm was too big. She used the correct one which showed that my pressure was normal. When I regained consciousness, she whispered, "Daddy, you're Shaheeba Barrow's husband. Yuh cyar go fainting dong de place!"

For some reason, people often assume I'm the doctor and Shaheeba is a housewife. Nothing could be further from the truth. Soon after we were married, my Dad dropped by our rented house and saw her mowing the lawn. I was in the kitchen with my apron, preparing lunch. He was old school and wasn't happy with this. He suggested getting together with Shaheeba's father and having a talk with her about being more domesticated. I would have loved to be a fly on the wall to hear how that went. Instead, I told him it was no problem, I didn't mind. Shaheeba must have heard me. I ended up cooking every day for the next 45 years.

A loans officer, seeing 'Dr. Barrow' on the application form, started to tell me about her vaginal discharge. It was too late to tell her she was talking to a pilot. To avoid embarrassment I had to go along with it. With my best bedside manner I asked, "So how long have you had this problem?" Meanwhile I wracked my brains to find an easy way out.

I used to attend medical seminars with Shaheeba, which were usually held at Chinese restaurants. While it's true I just went for the food, I did listen to the lectures. There was one on vaginal discharges by an eminent gynecologist. He said the first step in diagnosis is to get down there and take a good sniff. I looked at the elderly lady seated across from me, thought about it and said no way that's going to happen.

I seemed to remember something about douching with vinegar and water, and asked her if she ever tried that. She said no, but asked if it would help. I told her I had some success with it in the past. If not, some Draino should flush it down. She was very appreciative and thanked me for my professional services.

I was pleased with myself, and told Shaheeba about it when I got home. She said, "What? Vinegar and water? That's for cleaning carpets!" She also threatened to have me charged for practicing medicine without a license. I never heard from the officer again, so I assume my course of treatment was effective.

When Shaheeba's parents passed away, their property was divided amongst their four children. We decided to buy out the shares, renovate the house and put it up for rent. I placed an ad in the papers and made an appointment to see a prospective tenant. I went to the house a few minutes early to ensure that the workmen had left the place clean and tidy. With me was my dog, Bugsy, who insisted on going wherever I went. Like most cocker-spaniels, he was a bad-tempered SOB. He didn't read the part of the owner's manual which said a dog is not supposed to bite his master. I had to tread carefully with him.

Just as the family arrived, I was mortified to see that he had dumped an enormous pile of soft, smelly shit right in the middle of the living room. I started searching frantically for a towel to wipe it up, but the house was completely bare. In desperation I scooped it up with my hands and flung it out the window. I then rushed to the kitchen sink, only to find the faucet was dry. There was no water in the toilet bowl either!

By now the people were knocking and peering through the glass sliding door. Thankfully, I saw a bottle of Fabreze fabric cleaner on the counter. I sprayed some on my hands, wiped them on my jeans and greeted the family, who shook my hands. For some reason they didn't take the place.

<h1 style="text-align:center">Chapter 57</h1>

After finishing university I joined Terry and his German girlfriend Claudia in England. We set off on a two-month camping tour of Europe in his small Honda. We were on a tight budget and lived on French bread and potato chips, which we learned to say in several languages. In Marseilles I saw some meat in a deli which wasn't too expensive. I ordered a few grams and the woman laughed and said, "Pour le chien" (for the dog). That didn't faze me - I used to eat chicken feathers. She not only weighed the thin slice of meat but weighed the bread as well.

One 'meal' I refused was a can of tomato paste offered by some Arab guys in the tent next to mine. I'd seen them stirring some white powder in it and could only guess what it was. Drugs were readily available in Amsterdam so it could be anything. They insisted I try some, but I said, "No way - that's full of shit." Highly offended they said, "What you mean shit? This is good shit!"

Another time, in Belgium, I checked out the communal unisex showers. I put a 1 Franc coin in the heater and was enjoying a warm bath. Suddenly I heard a click and the water instantly changed to freezing cold. I came flying out of the shower stark naked, to the delight of the snickering crowd.

The high point of the trip was spending a morning in Rome. I visited the Coliseum, the Vatican Museum and the Cysteine Chapel. I'd seen the film 'The Agony and the Ecstasy' with Charlton Heston, and it was on my bucket list. I was mesmerized with Michelangelo's masterpiece which had recently been restored. Later I met up with Terry and Claudia, who were still drinking beer in the bar where I'd left them. They said there was nothing to see in Rome.

While back at Claudia's flat in Stuttgart I got a letter from my Dad addressed to 'Mr. Gerald Barrow, BSc.' I was surprised I'd gotten my degree. There had been riots on the St. Augustine campus during my final year, and we missed a lot of classes. His letter also stated that I'd gotten a job as a teacher at Malick Comprehensive School. I'd forgotten I'd applied for a teaching job. That was just a formality for every final-year student since a general science degree only qualified you to teach. My advice to all students is, "Do a course that has a proper job at the end."

Around that time the government had decided to do away with the 5-year school system. Instead, students would spend 3 years in a junior secondary school, and then switch to a senior secondary school to complete the last two years. They also introduced the shift system, in which each school would have one set of students in the morning and another in the afternoon. The idea was to give every child a secondary-level education, regardless of their SEA performance.

While it may have sounded great in theory it was the most disruptive thing imaginable. Children did little work in Junior Sec since there was no exam to pressure them. They then got into Senior Sec with just two years to prepare for CXC examinations. Also, the shift system meant that the morning students got out after lunch and had the whole afternoon to lime. It was no point going home since their parents would still be at work. I doubt the evening shift students learned much since a hot afternoon is the sleepiest time of day.

The results were predictable. While the denominational 5-year college students continued to excel, few shift system students got full certificates. It's no exaggeration to say that it screwed up an entire generation. One may argue that it's partially responsible for the present high crime rate in Trinidad since it's difficult to get meaningful employment without 5 CXC passes. After 30 years of failure, the government secondary schools are now changing back to the 5-year system.

Chapter 58

On my first day I drove around Morvant, a crime hot spot, looking for the school. I eventually found it down in a valley. The building was big and impressive, with the most modern equipment and facilities. 'Comprehensive' meant that both trade and academic courses were taught. The auto-mechanic students, for instance, had a fully equipped garage, complete with hydraulic lifts. Teachers took their cars there for a free service. The cooking students had stoves with modern overhead ovens. The art room had the most expensive brushes, paper and paints, most of which were discarded. You just had to sign up for the football team to get a full uniform, including free togs. In QRC our sporting implements consisted of an old bat and two stumps.

The first day was registration, and I noticed that many birth certificates were labeled 'Illegitimate'. They no longer do that, but it indicated that many of these kids didn't know who their fathers were. Most of them came from a nearby area called 'Never Dirty'. I could just imagine what that was like.

I was appointed Form Master of 4 Science, so was able to mold my class from day one. I started the camera club and taught them how to compose photos. I got Ministry financing to buy an enlarger, photographic paper and chemicals to equip the dark room. I divided the class into 5 groups and showed them how to develop film and print pictures. Each group had use of the room on a different day. With boys and girls in the room working till late, the principal was concerned about an adverse effect on the school population. Three of them went on to get jobs as newspaper photographers. I also organized field trips and used my boat to take them to the Gasparee caves. No way you can do that now.

Mine were a decent well-behaved bunch of students who I cared for. The same could not be said of the non-academic students. Many of them were budding anarchists with no interest in learning. I taught several different trade subjects, including electronics and machine shop science, but the job was basically that of a police constable.

A typical lab session would involve breaking up a basketball game, taking away the bongo drums and confiscating the money from the poker game. I'd be hoarse from shouting by the end of the day. I once had to supervise a typing class and there was a girl in front breastfeeding her baby. All the others crowded around, wanting one too. It was rumored that the plumbing teacher was the father. I don't know if that was true, but it sounded credible. Girls idolize their teachers, and there were a few 'smallies' who I knew had a crush on me. It takes a fair amount integrity to avoid the temptation.

Later, in the airline, captains would get 'current' from attractive flight attendants. The question they had to ask themselves was, "Is she really into me, or it is just because I'm the boss?" Us co-pilots never had that problem. No one gave us shit.

Chapter 60

I got along well with the other teachers, and we'd compare notes. One member of our close-knit circle was Nellisa, the geography teacher. Though frail and diminutive, she terrorized her charges, many of whom were twice her size. I admired her steely courage and fearless demeanor. She had more guts than me.

She was engaged to a bright but 'papesy' guy named Raj who worked in the oil industry. I was invited to their Hindu wedding by the sea. This was a colorful drawn-out affair, filled with obscure religious rituals and symbolism. Even the wedding date was decided by the Pundit, based on ancient astrological considerations. There were tassa drummers, with old tanties 'wining dong de place'. This was supposed to be a guide for the bride on her wedding night. I don't think Nellie needed any coaching. She was no spring chicken and had been round the block.

Nellie was not a Hindu but went along with the ceremony for the sake of her husband, Raj, who wanted to impress his expat bosses. At the reception the next day I was appalled to see her cheerfully serving her guests with one eye blackened. I asked her what happened, and she said that Raj cuffed her in her face. I said "What? But you just got married yesterday!" She said, "He told me he was going to give his mother my wedding gifts because she raised him from small. I told him why yuh doh go an fock yuh mudder one time, and he hit me." I said, "You know you deserved that, right?" She giggled and said, "True, but I couldn't let that one pass." She went on to have two beautiful, brilliant daughters, after which she got divorced. She said she just needed Raj for the sperm.

Meanwhile, the guys heard I had a boat and asked if I could take them fishing. I reluctantly agreed and told them to meet at my home on Friday at 7:00 pm. By 9:30 pm they had not arrived, so I figured they'd changed their minds. Around midnight I heard a tapping on my window. They were all outside and appeared to be drunk. It seems that the Moon River Club had just gotten a new consignment of Colombian women, and they stopped by to check them out. I was sleepy but had to get up and load the engine, gas tank, rope and anchor in my cousin's car.

When we got to Chaguaramas I had to swim out to where the boat was moored, row it in and put on the engine. We then drove to Scotland Bay and anchored there. None of the guys had ever fished before so I had to do everything. That included cutting up the bait and preparing the lines.

I told them that if they caught anything to hold it up over the side and see what it was before bringing it into the boat. Everyone was excited and soon began catching one crapaud fish after the other. These were ugly rockfish that were difficult to remove from the hook. Needless to say, I had to do that as well. Eventually, one of them caught a large moray eel, and, ignoring my instructions, flung it in the boat. It freed itself and started splashing around in the bilge. Everyone freaked out, thinking it was a snake. One of them grabbed an oar and started to fire blows at it. I had to grab it away before he smashed the boat to pieces.

Eventually, I managed to scoop it over the side. By then it was 4:00 am. I was drained and told them we had to go. They were disappointed, saying they were just starting to have fun. I noticed that the bottle of Johnnie Walker Black was now empty.

It was pitch black and we had no lights. As we cruised into the bay, I disconnected the gas line from the engine to drain the carburetor. The engine cut off and we coasted towards the shore. One guy named Dawg thought we'd reached and stepped over the side into the water. Fortunately, he was smoking a cigarette, so I saw the glow. I reached down into the blackness and managed to grab him by the collar. He emerged with the cigarette still in his mouth, too drunk to realize what had just happened.

I had to go through the reverse process of putting the engine in the car, rowing the boat out to its mooring and swimming back. By then dawn was breaking so I could see what I was doing. We got in Dawg's car, an old Corsair. Even though he was the most intoxicated, he had to drive since the car had side gear shifters which only he could operate. He also wanted to show us how fast it could go. So there we were, careening down the road with a drunken driver doing eighty-plus. Every now and then he'd vomit through the window, and we'd get sprayed in the back. Every time he retched, we'd have to duck. I swore, never me again. On Monday they told everyone what a great time they had, and asked when I could take them again.

Chapter 60

My penthouse apartment.

I spent a year at Malick and needed to get out. Up until then I was still trying my best, and didn't want to become blasé and crude like the others. One guy named Batson, who had been teaching for 22 years, was clearly over the edge. He once came into the class and saw a girl sitting on his desk. He told her to get her source of income off of it. I also heard him tell a boy that the only difference between you and shit is the color. I asked him how he could speak to the children like that. He said that's how they're spoken to at home, and it's the only thing they understand.

My cousin Johnny joined the staff, a prime example of a brilliant guy with a general degree who was only qualified to teach. I told him about the hooliganism in the school, but he dismissed my warning. He was into psychology and explained that these kids were from depressed homes and needed to be understood. Within a few weeks all that was out the window. At lunchtime, he'd bring a batch of miscreants into the staff room and beat the crap out of them. We'd beg him to take them outside – we were trying to eat.

Many years after I left he was still stuck there. I asked him how things were. He said, "Lemmee see. Yesterday a girl broke a desk over a boy's head, and another stabbed the VP in her stomach with a dividers. Same ole, I guess."

Sometimes I thought the girls were worse than the boys. Once, after lunch, I came into the class and found all the girls missing. I asked one of the boys where they were. He pointed through the window. There were some sweaty bare-backed workers digging a ditch at the side of the road with the girls gathered around them. I went outside and told them to get in class. They ignored me. One said, "Ay, res yuhself. Who you feel you is?"

My friend Kenrick was teaching at Woodbrook Secondary. He insisted that his hoodlums were worse than mine, and we'd make bets. He told me that, a few weeks before, he'd organized a field trip for his class to visit the pitch lake. Along the way the bus driver stopped to use a rest room. One of the students jumped in the driver's seat and drove off with the bus. The police found them later that night liming in bar in Cedros. They took them to the station to inform their parents. While waiting, another student grabbed the keys and they were off again. I had to admit he won that round.

There was a girl who I thought had some potential but wasn't applying herself. I asked her if she wasn't concerned about her future. She said, "Nar man, I cud get ah ten days on de project." By that she was referring to CEPEP, the Community-based Environmental Protection and Enhancement Program. This provides temporary employment for unskilled labourers. Long after leaving Malick I heard someone calling, "Sir, sir!" I knew from that mode of address that it must be a past pupil. I turned around to see a fat woman with a string-band of children. She looked familiar but I couldn't quite place her. I didn't want to ask her name, so I said, "Hi! How yuh going? What yuh doing with yuhself these days?" She beamed and said proudly, "I'm a checker on de project." "Ah," I said with recognition. It just shows that when you have drive and ambition the world is at your feet.

Like most of the other teachers, I spent my free time checking the employment section of the classified ads. Things were getting hairy, with police making frequent drug busts in the school. One teacher kept a sharpened pencil in his pocket. If attacked by a student, he said he'd stab him in the throat. That way he couldn't be charged with using a deadly weapon.

I applied for everything that would get me out of there. I once submitted an application for the manager of a glue factory. I told them I was always interested in glue. Under 'Previous Experience' I listed all the things I'd stuck – shoes, envelopes, etc. They never got back to me.

I also applied for the post of Chemist at WASA, the Water and Sewerage Authority. This time I made sure to be better prepared. I went to the headquarters in El Socorro, where the supervisor showed me around. I took notes on water extraction, purification and distribution. There wasn't a thing about water I didn't know. I walked into the interview room brimming with confidence. The first question they asked was what I did I know about sewerage. SHIT!

While at Malick, I lived in a dilapidated apartment building in Curepe owned by a slumlord named Narine. I was trying to save money, so the cheap $80 rent came in handy. Every now and then he would add new rooms or subdivide old ones. He would also cut the electricity to save on his light bill. I had the upstairs room, above the filth and squalor. He called it the Penthouse Suite.

One night a tenant I knew only as 'Breds' told me that his friend, Ras, was sick and needed to see a doctor. He was shaking, confused, and looked in a bad way. We put him in my car and, as I was driving towards the hospital, Breds said, "Not dat kinda doctor". Instead he directed me up a narrow valley in the northern range to the home of an obeah man named Papa Za.

Obeah men are spiritual healers who use herbs, rituals and a belief in supernatural powers. Papa Za sat Ras on a stool surrounded by candles of various colors. He waved incense and garlic and sprinkled him with rice and periwinkle flowers soaked in water. While doing so he chanted in tongues to drive out the evil spirits. After a while Ras calmed down and became lucid. The transformation was amazing. He was back to his old dopey self. I gave the doctor five dollars and thanked him for the consultation. I sometimes drive past Narine's place and marvel how my life has changed. No one can say I got things easy.

Chapter 61

Wedding Day, June 30th 1976

One night, after liming late with my friends, I met Mr. Maraj. He lived opposite my dad's house in Valsayn and had just come home as well. He worked in some Ministry and told me that the government would soon be offering scholarships in pilot training. If interested I should look for an ad in the papers and apply. Of course, I was interested. I was so desperate to get out of Malick I would have been happy scrubbing down the planes. Surely enough, a small notice did appear a few days later advertising the scholarships. If Mr. Maraj hadn't given me the heads up, I never would have seen it.

I put in an application with little hope. I was told that there were already four hundred applicants for the twenty places. A few months earlier, the BWIA pilots had gone on strike. They did so during the peak Carnival Season which angered the Prime Minister, Dr. Eric Williams. He decided to teach the white boys a lesson. He closed down the airline and fired all the pilots.

In those days almost every pilot was white. That's because only the 'French Creoles' could afford the high cost of training. It was a way to earn a good salary without having high academic qualifications. By offering scholarships Williams hoped to put some color in the cockpit.

My sister Daphne was a flight attendant. To prepare me for the interview she arranged for me to talk to a pilot friend who lived opposite. Like everyone else he was fired. He was very bitter because he was on leave at the time, and hadn't gone on strike. As such, much of the information he gave me was very critical of the airline, and the new DC9-50's that had been ordered.

There was talk that McDonald Douglas had bribed certain government officials to buy that aircraft. It was designed for domestic operations and unsuitable for our long-haul routes. I went into the interview room, not knowing that two of the people fingered were on the panel. With each question they asked I repeated what the pilot told me, which got them more and more angry. By the end they were actually shouting at me.

I was therefore most surprised when, not only had I won a scholarship, but was in the first group of ten. Having flown with my father had paid off. The second group would start 6 months later.

At that time I'd been asked by Frontiers Foundation to lead a group in British Columbia. My previous project was in northern Ontario, and I really wanted to see the west coast. I also wanted to be a better leader than Kyle, and make sure that everyone had a positive experience. I'd just gotten married, and Shaheeba was also going on a project in the nearby Yukon. If I dropped out, she'd have to go on her own. Also, if I left my job to start flying school, I'd lose my teacher's salary since I wouldn't have completed a full year of government service,

The scholarship paid $150 per month and my rent was $500. Shaheeba had started med school in Jamaica, and we were living off our savings. After getting her degree in zoology she taught for a year at Holy Name Convent, a Muslim teaching in a Catholic school. The money I saved by living in my penthouse would come in handy. We'd also found ways of supplementing our income. She would sew handbags with funny faced embroidery, while I would make the wooden handles out of polished mahogany. We'd go door to door selling them for $10 each. Her sewing skills also came in handy for our wedding. Up until a few hours before the ceremony she was still working on her wedding dress.

I am sometimes dismayed at how much people spend on weddings. It's all about status and trying to impress the other side. For our wedding there was no bamboo tent and no tassa drummers with old tanties wining. Instead of hiring caterers, Shaheeba's Mom cooked her signature stewed chicken, red beans and rice, which everyone enjoyed. I was the DJ and put on a belly- dancing record called 'Ya Habibi' which I enjoyed. The wedding cost next to nothing, and all our distinguished guests had an enjoyable evening. I gave her $500 dowry which I borrowed back next day to pay the rent. The honeymoon was spent that night at a nearby hotel. 50 years later we're still together. That's what I call value for money.

My gardener's son had gotten engaged to a girl down south. I offered to buy him a stove, which he appreciated. His father asked me for some financial assistance. I told him I was planning to buy a stove, but, if he preferred, I'd give him the $3,000 cash instead. He said he actually needed $20,000. That got me 'ignorant'. I said, "You want to buy rum and roti for the whole village to let everyone think you're a bigshot? This time your son doh even have a bed to sleep on!"

My Dad had once told me, "Before you find a place to rest your cock, find a place to rest your head." I was about six years old and thought he was talking about chickens. He was a cynical person, especially where finance was concerned. His favorite song was "Love is a Money Spending Thing." He would often quote Confucius saying, "Good ting no cheap - cheap ting no good!" My wife said I took after him, which I thought was a compliment. However she sent our boys to Hillview College rather than QRC, saying she didn't want them to turn out like me.

Chapter 62

Cessna 172

As for my flying course, the temptation was strong to place myself in the second group. A cocky guy, who I didn't like, somehow heard that I was contemplating making the switch. He called and asked if I could give him my place. I decided then and there to stick with the original plan, despite the sacrifices. That was a good thing since the strike was resolved and most of the pilots were rehired. As such, none of the students on the second course ever got jobs. I would have been back in Malick with a useless pilot's license in my pocket.

Despite the deprivations, having the government finance my training was a godsend. No way my father was paying for that. I completed the course in record time and was hired by BWIA, our national airline, the following day. For a more realistic chronicle of what's involved in becoming a pilot, I highly recommend 'The Courage to Fly' by my esteemed colleague, Captain Wendy Yawching.

Flying school was a trip, to say the least. There were 10 of us, including some foreign students from Aruba and Curacao. They were multilingual and we learned to cuss in Spanish, Dutch and Papiamento. When it comes to cussing, pilots put sailors to shame.

Our School was the Caribbean Aviation Training Institute, or CATI, based in Wallerfield and Mausica. Apart from us student pilots, there were engineers, firemen and avionics guys. Our classes were divided into one day of ground school followed by one day flying. The ground school subjects included navigation, meteorology, radio aids, flight planning, chart plotting, performance and law. For once I was doing something practical and interesting. As such I excelled, topping the class in everything.

We were given 10 hours of flying instructions after which we'd do our first solo. While in the circuit, the guys on the ground would be mixing a tub full of every vile liquid they could find, including old car oil, canal water, beer and detergent. After landing you'd be drenched and have to 'wear' this concoction for the rest of the day.

From then on we'd do our flying in pairs without an instructor. My partner was Joe, a nut case if ever there was one. With the three other planes in the air, we'd have dog-fights over the east coast. We'd switch radio frequencies so the Piarco air traffic controllers wouldn't know what we were up to. We each had 'handles', like 'Charlie Brown' or 'Black Sheep', in case anyone was listening in. I was 'Muddy Duck', which is now my internet password.

Joe was a curious guy. If he saw a car parked in a cane field, he'd want to know what was going on. As such he'd dive down low to try and peek in the windows. Back at the base, the mechanics would be puzzled by the cane leaves stuck in the wheels.

One of the exercises we practiced was a simulated engine failure. At some point during the flight the PNF (person not flying) would cut the engine. The flying pilot would then have to choose a suitable place to do an emergency landing. Since the plane was gliding without power he'd have to judge his turns properly to ensure he'd reach the field. At 500 feet you'd ask him if he thought he'd make it, then restore power.

Once, over La Brea, I cut the engine on Joe. He maneuvered the plane for a forced landing on the pitch lake. At 500 feet I asked him if he thought he would make it. He said, "Let's see." Oh no, this wasn't going to end well. As we came down, we saw a backhoe digging up the asphalt. The driver looked up and saw this Cessna 172 bearing down on him. He got out and started to run, with Joe following close behind.

A few years later, while flying on the 707, I heard a 'MAYDAY!'' call from one of my CATI instructors. He was a bush pilot from New Zealand and was a little informal when it came to standard operating procedures. He'd heard a distress call from a Korean fishing boat off the east coast. He'd jumped in a plane, probably without checking the fuel, and located the vessel. However, on the way back, he ran out of gas. He declared an emergency and did a forced landing on Manzanilla beach. The plane was fine but, in salvaging it, the mechanics disassembled it completely. I found out later that was for insurance purposes. With the plane in pieces the insurance investigators would be hard pressed to say that the incident was due to pilot error.

There was one instance when the insurers 'took infront'. There was a cricket match in St. Vincent, and my brother-in-law, Ian, and his friends chartered a small plane to go and see it. At the last minute something came up and Ian couldn't go. Just as well, since the plane crashed in the sea after takeoff, killing all on board. The water was very deep, but the insurance company hired divers who were first on the scene. I'm told that they 'found' that the fuel selector was off, meaning that the pilot had made an error. That absolved them from all liability.

Chapter 63

Every few months we'd have a flying exam. That entailed navigating along a route, correcting for wind speed and direction, and arriving at your destination within three minutes of your ETA (Estimated Time of Arrival). I decided to practice my route the day before my exam to familiarize myself with the landmarks, a good way of cheating. A storm was closing in from the east and the other guys scurried back to base. I figured I could complete my route before it hit. I was wrong. Soon, I was in the most severe turbulence I'd ever experienced. There was thunder and lightning, and the plane felt as though it was being hit by a pile driver. I began to wonder what glue Mr. Cessna used to stick the wings.

We had a bad weather procedure in which you would fly along the east coast to the Matura River, then head west to our base in Waller Field. I tried that but the plane wasn't moving. I could see the ground below me, and even though my airspeed was 90 knots I was still over the same tree. I was basically in a hurricane.

The CFI (Chief Flying Instructor), an Englishman named Mr. Courtney, was concerned and called me on the radio. I had difficulty answering because the microphone kept flying out of my hand. I told him I was somewhere over the Aripo savanna, which gave him the impression that I was lost.

He and a senior student pilot got into the twin Cessna 310 and found me, still over the same tree. Being instrument rated, he told me to follow him in but that was not possible due to the poor visibility. After a while, the wind died down a bit and I was able to make it back home. All my friends, who were anxiously following events on the radio, were convinced I was crazy. It seems the Cree children were right after all.

Joe had gotten his girlfriend Gemma pregnant. He was an insanely jealous guy. He was convinced she was having an affair with her gynecologist due to her frequent visits to his office. He also though she was having an affair with Donny, one of our fellow pilots, who dropped her home from church. Years later, when our friend Shaz had to do an upgrade check on

Donny, Joe told Shaz to 'buss' (fail) him. Shaz said, "Joe, you know I can't do that if he flies well." Joe said, "Shaz, yous meh fren or not?"

Gemma eventually had a healthy baby boy, but after a bitter break-up, she refused to let Joe see his son. I had a car and he asked me if I could take him to her house in St Augustine. I did so and waited outside. A while later he came running out shouting, "Drive, Drive!" He jumped in the car, baby in hand, with Gemma and her mother screaming and banging outside. He could have mentioned he was getting me involved in a kidnapping case.

The one downside of the school was the food. Most of the students boarded there and had to eat whatever was served. The caterer was a Guyanese guy named Blake who must have forged his food badge. There were frequent power outages in Mausica, during which the meat in the freezer would defrost and spoil. Once the power came back and it re-froze, he figured it was good to go.

People were getting sick. You'd see twisted aluminum food trays and spaghetti dripping from the walls, an indication of the dissatisfaction with the meals. After several complaints the principal established a 3-man committee, representing each course, to monitor the food situation. Even though I was married and cooked my own food at home I was chosen to represent the pilot body.

One day the guys brought me a jug of Kool Aide with maggots swimming around. I took it to the principal. He was Guyanese and a personal friend of Blakie, so just shook his head. Courtney got involved. He said that if you found worms on your plate you just had to move them aside. I told him I didn't know much about English cuisine, but we Trinis preferred our food without the maggots.

Chapter 64

Being on scholarship was a precarious thing. I was warned by Mr. Archibald, the only local instructor, that those who stuck their necks out could get their heads cut off. He was an ignorant man and had already thrown one student off the course.

Eventually, Archibald replaced Mr. Courtney as CFI. CATI was funded by the ICAO, the International Civil Aviation Organization. Its mission was to train local pilots as instructors to replace the highly paid foreigners. The problem was that, as fast as students graduated, they pursued lucrative jobs in the airlines rather than remain as instructors. Archibald was therefore put in charge to prove that we were going local. He had been an instructor at the Light Airplane Club forty years before and had taught my Dad to fly. Now, in his eighties, he was clearly going senile.

His first briefing as CFI went something like this. "You must always have your map. It's like a nudist walking down Frederick Street. I mean, you can swing a monkey by the tail and eventually it will get the banana, but you must always have your map." We stared at him in disbelief while Mr. Courtney simply stood, arms folded, with a bemused smile on his face. This was his replacement.

Mr. Archibald was responsible for training the foreign guys, but had one local student, my friend Shaz. He and Joe were responsible for many of the strange things that went on at the school. They once took all the bed sheets, rolled them into a big ball and threw it in the bush. The long-suffering cleaner, seeing the beds bare, went and complained to the principal. She dragged him to the dorm, only to find all the sheets back in place. He just shook his head and returned to his office, leaving the poor woman dumfounded.

Shaz desperately wanted to get out of Archibald's group. While we had excellent instructors from the UK, Switzerland and New Zealand, he was stuck with Arch. He felt as though, while were getting ahead, he was moving backwards. He would secretly ask the other instructors for a switch, but invariably Arch would find out. He would call Shaz into his office and ask, "Shageer, I hear you want to change instructors. What's the matter, you don't like me?" Poor Shaz would have to say, "No Mr. Archibald, I like you very much."

Eventually he gave up and decided to wait out the 6-month period, after which there would be a mandatory change of instructors. Arch came in with the list, and we all breathed a sigh of relief when we heard we wouldn't be with him. Arch ended by saying "And, in closing, I'll be keeping my old student, Shageer." Shaz's head hit the desk with a thud, while I laughed till I cried.

At this time Shaheeba was studying medicine in Jamaica and I decided to sneak out and spend a few days with her. I told my other friend Carl to cover for me since I'd be missing some classes. I also released her pet tarantula which she had found on a zoology field trip. I used to put cockroaches and grass hoppers in its cage every night and wasn't sure how long I'd be away. As such I let it out on the banana tree at the back of our rented house.

Donning my student pilot's uniform I got a free jump-seat ride and spent the weekend with her. We checked into a posh hotel in Ocho Rios where the receptionist wanted to charge us the foreign rates because we were not Jamaican. After living in Kingston for two years I knew the various types of 'clart' – blud, rass, bumba, pussy, etc. I offloaded a choice selection on her, and she promptly gave me the local rate.

We had a lovely time, sitting on the balcony of the top floor overlooking the sea. Below, they started grilling steaks, and the smoky aroma filled our nostrils. There was no way we could afford that. Instead, we opened our can of tuna and ate it with a slice of bread. That would be our dinner. I swore that one day I too would have a steak. Right now my freezer is filled with Choice US rib eyes. I never forget the days when we had to do without.

Back in school I was summoned into Archie's office to explain my absence. I said, "I was sick, sir". He watched me suspiciously and said, "But you look tanned!" I replied, "That's because I had roasting fever." Would you believe he swallowed that?

A few weeks later I was lying on my living room floor listening to the Carpenters when I felt something crawling on my chest. I turned on the lights and saw a flock of little spiders walking around. What was the chance of my tarantula finding a mate on the banana tree? I wrote Shaheeba about it and she said that tarantulas were hermaphrodite. They had both male and female sex organs and didn't need to mate.

Frantically, I ran out the back and started chopping down the banana tree. All of a sudden, this big black tarantula jumped out. It had grown to an enormous size. I didn't want to kill it. Instead I called my landlord and gave notice that I'd be leaving at the end of the month. I didn't bother to give a reason. I am a man of few words - you know, the strong silent type.

Shaheeba passed her exams and returned home as a qualified doctor. Around this time she became pregnant with my first son Mickhaiel. She was deathly afraid of labor pains, and managed to get her own bottle of trilene gas. Sometimes there was a shortage at the hospital, and she wasn't taking any chances. For 3 months the heavy cylinder remained in the trunk of her car, banging and rolling around.

When it was time for the delivery it was amusing to see her being wheeled into the room, clutching her cylinder for dear life. That's when she was told that the hospital had no masks! The nurses managed to find a small portable bottle, which I had to put over her face every time there was a contraction. Without a proper fit, I was breathing in as much gas as she. This went on for 14 hours. By the time Micky was ready to come into this world his papa were stoned.

Chapter 65

BWIA Boeing 707

Our course lasted 18 months and I passed all subjects with flying colors. I was halfway through my multi-engine training when BWIA announced that they were hiring pilots. Mr. Courtney must have put in a good word because I was called for an interview. I was told that the course would be starting in two weeks and if I could finish my training by then I'd be hired. I flew three times a day, morning, noon and night. I made up the 55 hours in time and was sick and exhausted by the end. I started training on the Boeing 707, the only one in my class ever to do so.

I was fortunate to work for our national airline, BWIA, during what I consider to be its golden years. During the shutdown, many of the senior captains left and went to fly with Singapore Airlines. From what I was told, some of these old 'colonials' were racists or just plain difficult. The ones that remained included some of the finest pilots in the sky. This was reflected in 'BWee' having a 100% safety record, a claim few other airlines could make.

Even though you had to be an instrument rated pilot to be hired, you didn't get to fly a plane for several years. New recruits started on the 'panel' as a flight engineer or 'P3', either on the Boeing 707 or Lockheed L1011. You 'sat sideways' and managed the aircraft systems, such as fuel, air-conditioning and pressurization, electrics, etc.

The first things a new pilot learns when coming on line are:-

1.   You don't mess with the captain's woman.

2.   You never know who the captain's woman is.

New crew members were often subjected to some sort of initiation prank on their first flight. Flight attendants would be sent outside to kick tires to check the pressure. Pilots might be asked to get a bucket of prop-wash or a right-handed screw driver.

On my first flight into NY, I heard a late night knock on my door. Standing outside was our gorgeous purser, Bobbie. No way I was that lucky – not on my first flight anyway. Suspecting that something was amiss, I refused to let her in. Good call. I found out next day that she was supposed to get me in a compromising position. The rest of the crew would then burst into the room and literally catch me with my pants down. I may appear dumb and naive, but that's just me, playing dead to catch corbeau alive.

The funniest prank I saw was when the F/O filled a bag with chicken noodle soup and placed it by his foot. He then 'dinged' the flight attendant and asked for a sick bag, saying he wasn't feeling well. She handed him the bag, and he bent over, pretending to throw up in it. He then switched bags and handed her the full one. The captain then grabbed the bag, saying, "Hey! That's good food!" He dipped his hand in and started stuffing the 'vomit' in his mouth. The F/A nearly vomited herself.

The most elaborate ruse was played by my friend John. He was the purser on a flight from London that was practically empty. The rookie F/A was a Veni guy named Joseph. He told Jose to do the meal service for two English girls seated at the back. After giving them their food, John told him that one of them was having difficulty breathing.

He grabbed an oxygen bottle and rushed to the back. Surely enough, she was gasping for breath. Her friend said angrily, "You gave her the fish! She's allergic to seafood!" She placed her friend on the floor, opened her blouse exposing her ample breasts, and told him to give her CPR. This he did for several minutes, alternating between chest compressions and mouth to mouth.

Eventually she started to recover. John told the Jose, who was shattered, that the captain wanted to speak with him. Fearfully, he opened the cockpit door and said, "Yes capitan?" The skipper reached back, shook his hand and said, "Welcome to Bwee." Puzzled, he went back to the cabin to find the entire crew, including the 'sick' girl, rolling with laughter. Finally clued in, he said tearfully, "John, you was shittin me!"

Other airlines have their pranksters. My friend, who flew for Pan Am, said they had a captain who would stumble out of the cockpit to use the washroom wearing dark glasses and holding a white cane. Another would put a rubber chicken on the windscreen when approaching the gate. His crew would chalk the numbers 1 to 10 on the nose wheel before takeoff. After landing, whoever guessed the number touching the ground would win the pot.

Our flights included overnights in Miami and three-day layovers in New York and Toronto. Those were the days before internet shopping, so we got a chance to buy things that were on the 'negative list'. Once, during Christmas, a customs officer confiscated a ham from a flight attendant. She did some checking and got his name and address. The next day, when he was on duty, she went to his home. She told his wife that her husband had offered to keep her ham for her. The wife said, "Yeah, I see he bring home something las night an put it in de fridge." She took the ham out of the refrigerator and gave it to its rightful owner.

On another occasion a customs officer heard a buzzing sound coming from a flight attendant's suitcase. Alarmed, he called security who gingerly opened the case. There they found her 12-inch vibrator which had turned on accidentally. She was an attractive girl, but the word went round that, if she ever came knocking on your door late at night, don't get excited - she just needs batteries.

Chapter 66

On a plane the captain is king. They have no respect for authority. On my first flight on the 707, as we were about to start, the ground engineer asked to hold on while they checked something. After a few minutes the General Manager, who was seated in first class, poked his head in the cockpit and said "Well, tell the passengers something." The captain spun around angrily and shouted, "Fock you!" That was his boss he was talking to. The GM put his tail between his legs and slunk back to his seat.

Once, between sectors, we were having breakfast and the agent started boarding without permission. The captain, Mike, told him to take the pax back to the gate. That included the Deputy PM. They had to wait until Mike finished his 'doubles' before re-boarding.

Later in my career, I refused a jump-seat ride for the airline's CEO, who was an arrogant little prick. On another occasion I had his firearm removed from the hold, just to piss him off. He told the flight attendant that he wanted to speak to me. I said I didn't want to speak to him. He had laid off many of my friends in a most callous manner, having them escorted out of the building by security with no warning whatsoever. Imagine going to work one day, then coming home an hour later to tell your wife you were out of a job. In some ways that defined my career. Khalid is still wary when asked at work, "Are you Gerry Barrow's son?"

Once, during a normal landing in Barbados on the 707, the nose wheel strut broke. The front of the plane dropped, and we went scraping along the runway. By the time we came to a halt, smoke began to fill the cabin. We had to do an emergency evacuation. Everything was handled expertly by our well- trained flight attendants, and no one was hurt.

Afterwards, all crew members were required to submit a written report. I gave a full account of the incident, including the damage I noted during my inspection. I later saw my report in a folder on the fleet manager's desk labeled 'A First-Class Report'. The Captain and First Officer, how-ever, had simply written "Landed in BGI and nose-wheel broke". When instructed to rewrite it they said the same thing. That bothered me. Did I do something wrong?

Years later, during a CRM (Crew Resource Management) course, I asked the American instructor about it. He said what the pilots did was correct. All accident reports should be as concise and vague as possible. The more you write the more likely an insurance investigator can find a reason to void your policy. Smart arse lawyers could also find you criminally negligent and sue the airline.

As such, after an incident, a crew's SOP (Standard Operating Procedure) is to erase the CVR (Cockpit Voice Recorder) and cook up a story to CYA (Cover Your Arse). There's a saying in the industry that, after an accident, if the pilot dies, it was his fault. If he lives, you'll never know what really happened.

To avoid having to do extra sectors while on the way home, a common practice is to pretend the radio isn't working properly. Pilots would key the microphone intermittently and tell the Ops Controllers, "Sorry, bzzzz bzzzz, you're breaking up, bzzz bzzz". It's said that scam goes all the way back to Marconi who invented the radio. I even saw a captain stuff cigarette foil into the phono jack to short circuit the radio. This grounded the plane, and saved him from doing an addition leg to Georgetown after returning from NY. He wrote in the logbook that the radio was 'NFG' (No Fucking Good.) Next day he was called into the Fleet Manager's office for posting an obscene entry. He said that NFG stood for 'Not Functioning Good.'

He was a crazy guy who burned up two turboprop engines after landing because his girlfriend, the stewardess on the flight, had jilted him. Cost to the airline was one million USD each. He chain smoked and lived on coffee, which I think created a chemical imbalance in his brain. While flying with him I'd have to wear my oxygen mask to protect my eyes and nose. After his wife filed for divorce, she brought a SWAT team to their home in Miami when she went to collect her belongings. He told me there were snipers in the grass, and he was puzzled why they needed two prison vans.

Around that time my Dad's mechanic, Harold, was also going through a divorce. When his wife, my siblings' piano teacher, came to collect her belongings, she brought along a policeman. Harold was very accommodating and allowed her to enter the bedroom. He then slammed the iron door shut and proceeded to chop her with a cutlass. The policeman could hear her screams but could do nothing. Harold then tried to slit his throat, but only managed to put a slight scratch on his neck. I guess it must have hurt. He was tried for her murder and died in jail.

Gender violence continues to be a major problem in Trinidad, as in many other parts of the world. As I see it, some reasons include :-

1. Men have this outdated notion that they are superior to women because they have more muscle mass. We are no longer hunter / gatherers, so big biceps mean nothing. Put men and women in a classroom and the females will outperform the guys every time. My old college, QRC, stopped taking in girls for A-levels because they said the girls were 'distracting' the boys, i.e., they were embarrassing them.

2. Men have this macho attitude that they are boss. They can come and go as they please, and do whatever they want. Wives are supposed to stay home and take that. Women are no longer content to just being housewives. They are educated, skilled and qualified. They don't need a man to tell them what to do.

3. Working wives bring in additional income, which helps to pay the bills. However, some men feel emasculated if their wives earn more than them. How stupid. My take is that, if my wife is not making more than me, she not working hard enough. If she's not smarter than me, what's the point of having her around? I need a competent partner, not some sex-pot gas-brained air-head.

4. Men are insecure. They are afraid that their women might stray if not kept under tight manners. To prevent this possibility, they cover them up and restrict their movements, Taliban style. The way I see it, women, unlike men, are genetically monogamous. Treat your woman right and she will remain faithful to you. If she leaves, you have only yourself to blame.

5. Cultural absurdities. The reason girls are not allowed to be educated past age 6 in certain fundamentalist cultures is because a woman is not supposed to be more knowledgeable than her husband.

Seeing that the average Islamist has an IQ of five and a half inches, that limits his wife's education.

6. Horn - that's our local word for being cuckolded. Women are materialistic because they need to provide for their kids. If she finds someone more motivated and affluent, she may leave your lame arse backside. What sense does it make killing her then killing yourself? Kill yourself first. We have a saying, "A horn is only a horn if you take it orn." Find someone else. There's plenty fish in the sea.

7. Hanging your hat higher than you can reach. Every man would love to lock down a sexy senorita, but these are high maintenance commodities, and you can get burned. She may be with you for now but she's scoping out the scenes. One BMW is worth two Tiidas, so adios gringo.

To quote the Mighty Sparrow :-

> *The one who you love, never marry to she.*
> *Is the one who love you, she go make you happy. Keep the one*
> *who you love on the side all the while.*
> *But the one who love you, take she straight dong the isle.*

I saw a recent news item in which Gambia has plans to reverse the ban on FGM (Female Genital Mutilation). And that's a modern progressive African nation. What the fuck century are we living in?

Chapter 67

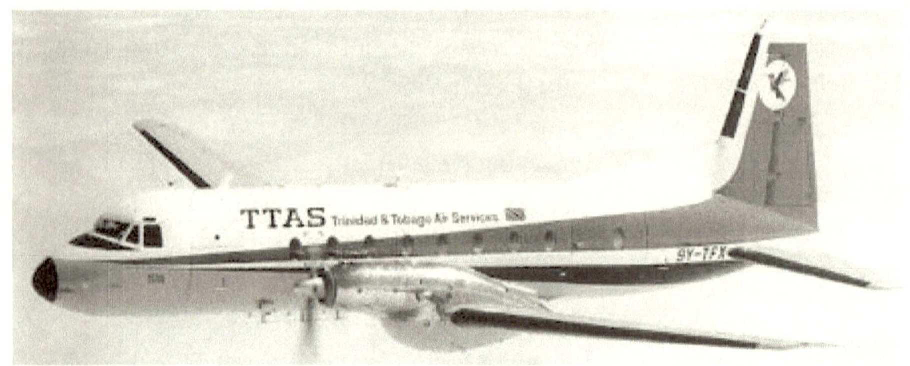

TTAS Avro

After serving three years on the 707 panel I finally got a chance to fly a plane. That was the HS 748 Avro, a post-war British relic which actually needed a shot of alcohol to get it off the ground. Not having had much handling practice, it was like learning to fly all over again. My fellow trainee was my big Laventille friend Clinton. The training involved doing 'touch and go' circuits in Piarco. We'd judge each other's landings by how many pieces of emergency equipment fell out of the overhead lockers. Once qualified, we flew eight sectors between Trinidad and our sister isle Tobago. Things were informal to say the least.

One morning, on the first flight to Tobago, we gave a jump-seat ride to an air-traffic controller. This was a common courtesy which saved them having to buy a ticket. Halfway across, the Piarco controller handed us over to Crown Point. We tried contacting the tower but got no reply. Eventually the guy in the cockpit owned up. "Skip, actually it's me that's supposed to be in the tower, but I missed my flight last night. Anyway, you're cleared to land, wind zero nine zero at ten knots, QNH 1013." The captain and I looked at each other incredulously. What a privilege! We had our own personal ATC on board.

Once, on the way back from Tobago, the flight attendant rushed into the cockpit and said that a woman had brought a bag of crabs on board.

The wet bag had burst, and crabs were roaming around the cabin. We looked back and saw passengers standing on their seats. "What should I do?" asked the distraught FA. The captain said, "Close the door behind you."

Strangely enough, most of my freaky incidents occurred on this short route. Once, while landing, the right wing suddenly flipped upwards. I jammed the throttles forward and did a go-around. While down-wind abeam the tower, I saw 3 whirlwinds moving across the runway. By now they had picked up dust and were clearly visible. I waited till they passed before attempting another landing. We pilots have a saying, "A good landing is one you can walk away from. A great landing is when they can still use the plane."

A frightening incident occurred one night during a departure. A storm was approaching from the east, and I wanted to get out before it hit. During the takeoff roll there was a flash of lightening and the whole airport went black, including the runway. Also, an intense downpour hit us, obscuring all visibility. It was like flying through Niagara Falls on a moonless night.

Committed to the takeoff, I slowly lifted the plane off the ground, trying to keep it straight in the severe turbulence. The Crown Point runway in those days had coconut trees on either side. The Avro had an abysmal rate of climb. As I watched the altimeter slowly creep up, I wondered how tall a coconut tree could grow. I knew they were close by but couldn't see a thing. Eventually, as we crept past 100 feet, I figured we should be clear. I could breathe again.

We did charters for LIAT, with 8 stops up the islands. We'd then over-night in St. Thomas, US Virgin islands, then do the same thing in reverse the next day. It was very exhausting. The airports in those days were very basic, and all the landings were quite hairy. Pearls in Grenada had a yellow line near the threshold. If you didn't get your wheels on the ground by then you'd end up in the sea. Our official procedure when going into Canefield Airport in Dominica was, 'Make a sharp left turn by the bread-fruit tree on the hill, then fly down the valley.' People on either side would wave at us from their living rooms as we passed below them.

One night I was having dinner in St. Thomas with a captain named Kemraj. Kemmy was a big-hearted guy, loved by everyone. His front door was open 24/7, and he would hide your keys until the bottle was finished. The restaurant was a small family affair. As the evening progressed and the alcohol went to his head, his voice got louder and his language deteriorated. With other guests glaring at us, I told Kemmy we should keep it down. He said it was okay, since the local lingo was different from ours. I said that kind of language was universal. To prove his point he shouted to the waiter across the room, "Ay, yourmuddercunt!" The waiter said, "Yes sir?" Kemmy asked, "You understand what I just called you?" "No sir," said the waiter. Kemmy exclaimed, "You see? Dey doh know one fock I say!"

Tragically, Kemmy was stabbed in the neck while defending his mother during a home invasion. At his Hindu cremation at the Caroni River, a Bwee jet flew overhead, rocking its wings in silent tribute.

We had an eccentric captain of Dutch descent who had a good head for business. To take advantage of various shortages up the islands, he would go into the terminal at each stop and peddle various house-hold products. Passengers would be waiting on board while he hawked his bleach and detergent. Eventually, the exasperated station managers would make announcements over the PA, "This is a final boarding call for Captain Petersen. Please proceed to the aircraft immediately!"

He had a brother, Jan, who had the same financial proclivity. One night on the 707, we were on final approach into Toronto. The weather was marginal, with fog and blowing snow. As we descended towards our minimum approach altitude the Captain and I were straining our eyes to spot the approach lights. If we didn't go visual by 200' we'd have to do a missed approach and proceed to our alternate, Buffalo. Jan was the First Officer, and I noticed that his head was down. Things were tense and I though he was praying. On closer inspection I realized that he was counting US!

Chapter 68

BWIA MD 83

To save money, airline manufactures often 'stretch' an existing aircraft to accommodate more passengers rather than design a new plane from scratch. This affects its performance, sometimes with disastrous results. No so with the MD-83, which was the stretched version of our DC9-50. They were the Ferrari's of the sky - you couldn't slow them down. We were one of the first airlines to get this new aircraft. They were the most modern planes in the world, with their multifunctional 'glass' displays and auto-land capability. I wanted to get my paws on one. The Bwee training department was a closed shop, which ensured that friends, family and 'brown-tongues' got promoted. I was 'None Of The Above.'

There was an elitist training captain who was appointed manager of the MD83 fleet. Called 'Captain O/O', for 'Owner/Operator', he considered the fleet to be his private country club. You needed the right pedigree to be admitted. I was 'bold-faced' enough to apply.

While on training, he insisted we wear suits in the simulator. To reduce costs, our 'sim' sessions were booked in the wee hours, and the dress code was casual. The Americans would often turn up in shorts and flip-flops. Having to wear 'court' clothes at 3:00 a.m. in a deserted building was ridiculous. What's even more inane is the custom whereby you have to leave the lower button of your jacket undone. I don't know who came up with that, probably Julius Caesar or some other Latino.

To annoy O/O I deliberately buttoned mine. That freaked out my friend and fellow trainee, Ryan. He was horrified and hissed, "Gerry! Your button!" I replied, "This is my 'effin' jacket and these are my 'effin' buttons." That did not go down well with O/O. I obviously lacked class and sophistication.

O/O was a keep-fit fanatic. Being his student, Ryan was obliged to go jogging with him, and had to pretend he enjoyed eating bran muffins for breakfast. Meanwhile, I'd deliberately order runny eggs and every grease-dripping item on the menu. I'd sop up the mess with buttered toast, hash browns and bagels with sour cream. Maybe I went too far, but WTF, that's just me. I never suck up to anyone.

During the next two days O/O did his best to trip me up in the 'sim'. That included pushing the throttles forward as I was getting into my seat, saying, "Let's go," before I did my checks. We were hurtling down the runway while I fumbled to fasten my seat belt and keep the plane straight.

There was method in his madness. One of the radio selector 'ears' on the instrument panel was in the wrong position. It was set to 'NDB' instead of 'VOR' for the SID (Standard Instrument Departure). I would have picked that up if I'd been allowed to do my checks, but that was the trap he set for me. I soon realized the error and corrected it before any harm was done.

Even though everything went well, he refused to sign my license. At the debriefing he said I was 'dangerous' for turning towards the wrong station after take-off, even though they were located next to each other. I prepared myself for more setups.

The last part of the training was the base check back at Piarco, in which we flew the real plane in the circuit. Once again, I flew perfectly, and once again he refused to sign my license, saying we had to talk. Talk about what? How best to take his fleet and shove it up his arse? That's what I was prepared to discuss.

It was Ryan's turn to fly next. When O/O failed the engine after take-off poor Ryan kicked the wrong rudder. The plane almost flipped on its back, fifty feet above the ground. O/O had to grab the controls to recover. I was wondering what we were going to talk about, seeing that the guy he trained nearly killed my tail.

In the debriefing room he reluctantly signed my book and flung it back at me. It didn't matter - I was now a qualified MD-83 pilot. I met Ryan in the car-park, still visibly shaken, and thanked him for saving my job.

Chapter 69

Strangely enough, O/O treated me very well after that. He'd bought a compound bow and, hearing I was into archery, wanted to use my target. Though I was required to follow every whim and fancy of the captain while on duty, there's nothing in our Ops. Manual which said I had to allow anyone into my home. As such, he had to shoot on his own. I'm a vindictive sonofabitch with a long memory.

I was a founding member of the Trinidad Archery Federation and used to help out with the youngsters. There was one snobbish guy named Gerard who didn't get involved in training. Instead, he'd set up his own target and shoot with his friend Simon. One day Simon asked me to join them. Gerard shot first, using his fancy Olympic recurve bow, which looked like something out of Star Wars. He took his time, adjusting for wind, humidity, and I don't know what else. He hit the target, which was set at 50 yards, but was nowhere near the yellow bull's eye.

Next it was my turn. I'd never shot at 50 yards but made no adjustment to my sight which was set for 30 yards. The tension on my compound bow was set at 60 lbs, enough to bring down a cape buffalo, so I didn't expect the arrow to drop by much. Sure enough I did hit the bull's eye, but just below the center. Gerard was stunned. He looked through his field telescope to see if it was true.

It was his turn again. This time he made adjustments for atmospheric pressure, the sunspot cycle, and the fact that it was a leap year. He took forever before shooting, as though waiting for the second coming. His shot was closer to the middle but still outside the yellow circle. Meanwhile, I lowered my pin slightly and hit the bull's eye, dead center.

Gerard was dumbstruck. He didn't trust the telescope and walked to the target to see for himself. There was a tiny cross right in the middle of the bull's eye, and my arrow was just off to the right. My son Micky, who was eight at the time, exclaimed "Daddy! You missed the X!"

Gerard took down the target, threw it in his truck and sped off. He never returned. I'd be the first to admit it was a lucky shot on my part, but it came at the right time.

Khalid and I practice shooting now and then. We'd put up a picture of a 'spranger' at thirty yards and call which body part we were going to hit. While I would go for a head or chest shot, he would choose an eye. His accuracy is unerring, and he always beats me on points.

When he brought in his bow from the States it was seized by customs. At that time archery was considered a sport. Not only was the equipment legal, but it was also duty free. I told him not to worry. Even though I was retired, I put on my old uniform, went to the airport and told a customs officer that they had my bow. The guy replied, "Sorry skip, we didn't know it was yours." Khalid couldn't believe when I emerged two minutes later with his bow in my hand.

Things have changed now. Anything remotely associated with archery, down to the string, is illegal. To import any equipment I'd have to prove I belonged to an archery association. As such, I invented an organization called the Trinidad and Tobago Archery Club. I used my graphics skills to design a logo and ID for the purpose. The abbreviation, TTAC, is the same as my genuine astronomy club, the Trinidad and Tobago Astronomy Club. Any Google check will show that the TTAC actually exists.

I'd applied for a FUL (Firearms User License) with the police many years ago, but my application was declined. It seems that only criminals are allowed to have guns. I still sleep with my bow at my bedside. If I see anyone in my yard at night, all you'd hear is the snap of the string. At 60 lbs tension, the arrow would go clean through the head and come out the back. I'd throw the body in my truck, tie a foundation block around a foot and dump it in the Caura river. The caimans would dish it up in no time. If my wife wakes up and asks if everything is okay, I'd say, "Yeah darling, no problem, go back to sleep." I like to keep things simple.

I certainly wouldn't inform the police. Their policy states that intruders have to be inside your house. You are only allowed to shoot them if they shoot at you first. I'd be charged for murder and my bow would be confiscated. I have a fake homemade bow handy for that purpose, made of bamboo and fishing line. I also have fake arrows made with dowel rods. They can keep those if they want.

I once made a fake M16 assault rifle for my daughter, Sofi. She had organized a fund-raising fashion show while at med school. The money raised went to finance the seniors' graduation ball, which she was tasked with organizing. The girls insisted that she modeled with them. Being a fan of the video game 'Call of Duty', she decided to go as 'Miss M16'. I made a replica of the rifle out of wood and aluminum, which included a laser sight. It was so realistic that Shaheeba insisted I destroy it right after the show in case I was held for possession. I took a photo posing with it before cutting it up. It's Sofi's favorite photo of her crazy Daddy, and hangs in her bedroom.

Chapter 70

There's a common notion that pilots and flight attendants have orgies in the hotels on layover flights. Unfortunately that is not so. Most crew members are in stable relationships and have no interest in a one-night stand. Besides, on NY and Miami flights, the priority is 'shop till you drop.'

Kingston flights were different since there wasn't much to do after eating your jerk chicken and 'festival'. Once, after checking into my room, I heard an urgent rapping on my door. I came out of the shower, wrapped a towel around my waist, and noticed an envelope on the floor. Puzzled, I picked up the envelope and opened the door. Before I could read the note the purser snatched it from my hand and said, "Wrong room." Our captain was an extremely handsome guy who was going through a divorce. The next day, on the bus, I noticed that the two of them were very cozy.

I spent 15 years flying DC-9 and MD-83 jets into Miami, NY and Toronto. These flights into high density airspace were intense and stressful, especially in the old days before modern autopilots and area navigation. Everything now is push-button automation, with the pilots doing little 'hands on' flying.

There is a joke which says that, in the future, there will just be a dog and a pilot in the cockpit. The dog is to ensure that the pilot doesn't touch anything. The pilot is there to feed the dog.

Pilots are known for shit talk. To be a good pilot you have to be a qualified shit talker. That's the only way you'll get through the long flights. Once, Bwee's management decided to hold a course on 'The Use of English'. They were not happy with the green verbs used by pilots during their PA announcements. Of the 50 guys rostered, only two showed up, me and my friend Stephen. This was going to be fun since Stephen was the biggest shit talker of all time. The woman started by asking him what was his definition of stress. Steven, in his usual laconic drawl, said, "Marm, stress is when yuh cast net buss an all yuh jashwar fall out." The poor woman stared at him dumbfounded. Things went south after that. No more English courses were ever scheduled.

Flying international routes into high density areas could be stressful, and there were scary moments. One such incident occurred on a flight out of Kingston. We landed in Puerto Rico and the sniffer dog found 24 cases of compressed marijuana in the hold. The aircraft was impounded, and we nearly spent the night in jail. I'm told the airline had to pay millions to get back their plane. Around that time my small, timid friend, Joe, was detained at JFK on terrorism charges. It took a long time for him to be cleared, a case of mistaken identity. It seems that 'Joe' was a common name amongst Islamic Jihadists.

On another occasion I was lined up on the runway in Piarco on a flight to Guyana. Suddenly all the runway lights went off. I informed the controller in the tower. He calmly replied, "The airport is closed. We just got a report that Abu Bakr has staged a coup, and Libyans are on the way." I said okay and informed the passengers that we'd be returning to the gate.

While flying over the Bahamas, a passenger once asked the flight attendant the name of the island we were passing over. She looked through the window and said, "Dilligaf". I was impressed, since there are over a thousand islands and keys in the archipelago. I asked her how she knew. She said that 'Dilligaf' stood for, "Do I Look Like I Give A Fuck?"

Chapter 71

I flew with the airline for over thirty years. During that time I was accepted by the various cliques. Being of mixed race, the white guys considered me white, and the black guys considered me black. Keith and Daphne lived in West Moorings, so, by osmosis, I was absorbed into that exclusive community. Having a boat gave me leeway into the rich boys 'Down the Islands' lime. I was an all-rounder.

Not being a drinker, however, was a major setback. After arriving at the hotel in NY, the various crews were expected to meet in the bar downstairs. I'd quietly order a 7-Up with an olive and pretend it was a martini. Once assembled, the guys would slowly drink one beer after the other and 'mauvaise langue' their friends and colleagues. Whoever left would be the next topic.

I'd be bored stiff as I nursed my cocktail for hours on end. By the time they were ready for dinner the restaurants would be closed. I'd have to go to bed starving. Eventually I said, "F dat" and didn't bother to lime with the crews. Let them bad-talk me if they wanted. Instead, I'd order takeout Chinese and watch CNN in my room until I wound down and fell asleep. I didn't give a shit what anyone thought. I was always a non-conforming individualist and did my own thing.

If you ever see a movie in which there's an emergency and the pilots are frantic, that is BS. We are the coolest guys in the world. Ask my wife. Cockpit voice recordings show that pilots remain calm even in the face of death. One Turkish Airlines co-pilot even told his captain, "Goodbye Papa" just before they crashed.

I'm always baffled why people are afraid to fly. You're safer in a plane than when driving to the airport. Besides, dying in a plane crash is more thrilling than lung cancer, heart failure or stage 3 lyme disease. You'll make the news. My personal preference is a high speed collision on my motorbike with a gasoline tanker.

There's a joke in which a plane was about to crash. The Trini captain told the French First Officer, "We have two parachutes. You take one and I'll take the other." The F/O asked, "But vot about ser hostess?" The Trini said, "Marn, fock she." The Frenchman replied, "But vill ve have time?"

Chapter 72

Every six months pilots have to renew their license with a flying exam. Two grueling days are spent in the simulator in which everything goes wrong, starting with an engine failure after takeoff. You never get back the engine for the rest of the two-hour flight. During that time you are expected to handle all emergencies while flying the route and 'shooting' the approach with absolute precision. Afterwards, anything that can happen on a real plane is something you've dealt with many times before.

Check rides are very subjective things. You could be failed for any reason, including personal grudges, and have little recourse. Everyone knows from before who's going to get through and who's going to 'buss'. If you repeated with another training officer he would be reluctant to pass you since it was his 'pardner' who failed you. Two fails and you were out of a job.

The most dreaded exams for first officers were the annual Route Checks. These were done by fellow F/O's with managerial aspirations, hoping to make a name for themselves. Giving you a bad report would show that their standards were higher than yours. It was also an opportunity to settle scores, and 'spirit-lash' was the order of the day. During a normal flight you could be asked question on anything from the many manuals, including the engineer's. This was unfair since we were only required to memorize the emergency procedures in the QRH (Quick Reference Handbook). It was so stressful that one of my friends had to seek psychological help after a check.

I once pulled a ratch. The training officer on the flight was my old friend Shaz. I gave him a list of topics which I'd prepared. However, during the flight, he was asking me stuff I didn't know. Realizing that something was wrong, he checked his folder and realized he was using the wrong list!

Another friend, called 'Honey' by his flight attendant wife, decided to secretly record the questions asked on the flight. He transcribed them and took the list to the CAA. They were appalled, and gave instructions that pilots were not to be distracted while operating. Reluctantly, the training guys just had to sit quietly and observe, which was in fact their function. The rest of us were ecstatic. Even though Honey denied making the recording, we changed his name to 'Grammy', for Best Recording by an F/O during a Route Check.

Chapter 73

Tobago Express Dash 8

My last few years were spent flying regionally with our sister airline, Tobago Express. This allowed me to sleep every night in my own bed with my own wife. Being in this work-friendly environment, I got involved in many crew activities. I took photos of our beautiful flight attendants and made an 'Employee of the Month' calendar. The fleet manager hung a copy in his office and was always anxious to receive the latest pin-up. Some of the girls used these photos to get modeling jobs. I also helped organize tourist tours, wrote the Rules and Regulations hand-book, organized the vacation roster and designed the logo for the TABEX cargo service.

I was chairman of the Tobago Express pilots' union at the time. One night, while flying over Northern Range, the first officer complained that we should be getting hazard pay. He said, "If we crash, you know how much big snake dey have dong dey?"

Caribbean Airlines Dash 8

Later, Caribbean Airlines absorbed TABEX. Dash 8 routes with CAL included the windward islands, Caracas, Guyana and Suriname. Our schedule into the latter two were in the wee hours of the morning when there was often fog. For the flight into Timehri, Guyana, the alternate was Piarco. This meant you had enough reserve fuel to return home if the airport was closed. When overnighting in Georgetown, Guyana, the engineers would close the doors of the aircraft and sleep inside This was to prevent the large white snakes that frequented the airport from crawling up the steps.

One night, on touchdown, I saw two dogs on the runway. One of them started to run but the other just stood and stared. Unable to do anything about it I hit him with a thud. On my walk-around inspection all I found was an ear. The rest had vaporized.

Flights to Zanderij, Suriname, were critical. It was too far south to get back to Piarco. If you couldn't land there, the alternate was Timehri, which might be fogged in also. What did you do then? There was nothing but dense jungle for hundreds of miles. On the way to Suriname I'd always pass over Timehri to see for myself what it looked like. If it was foggy I'd turn around and head back home. Fortunately it never came to that.

Chapter 74

Shaheeba talking to a Berber in the Sahara

I retired early at age 58, hoping to have some time to devote to my many interests before pre-senile dementia kicked in. I was already halfway there. These interests included wine tasting, music, and scanning my extensive coin collection, which I considered to be a five-year development plan. There were also a few more interesting places we wanted to see.

Shaheeba is an inveterate traveler who likes to visit exotic destinations, especially middle-eastern countries. There she gets to practice her Arabic, which she speaks with a Trini accent. While touring Yemen, the travel company supplied us with a guard armed with a Kalashnikov AK-47 assault rifle. Four German nurses were murdered in that area a few days before, and they were taking no chances.

Driving through the desert we stopped to have lunch with some Bedouin nomads at their camp. We ordered the goat and soon after the cook walked pass with a goat's head in his hand. Since there was no refrigeration, all meat was freshly prepared. After the meal I went to use the make-shift washroom and was followed by the guard. When Shaheeba,

Sofi and our house-keeper, Jess, went, he didn't accompany them. I asked him why, and he replied, "They're just women."

On another trip to Kashmir we were stopped by Pakistani border guards. Pakistan was at war with India at the time and we looked like Indians. On checking our passports they said they never heard of Trinidad and Tobago. When I told them that's where Brian Lara was from, they immediately lit up and let us through. After that we just had to say, "Lara" at every roadblock and get royal treatment. Brian would be pleased to know he's well regarded in the Himalayas.

While visiting the Dome of The Rock in Jerusalem, the Palestinian guard pointed a machine gun at us and told us to recite verses from the Koran to prove we were Muslim. That was no problem for my wife and kids who went to the TML Muslim school in St. Joseph. They, however, looked at me with some trepidation. Being a non-religious guy, they were anxious to see what I would do. Looking down the barrel of an AR 15, I suddenly remembered the verses I was required to recite when getting married. I quoted these and was allowed to pass. My daughter said with relief, "Daddy, now I can believe anything."

While entering Jerusalem we were detained by Israeli border guards and questioned for several hours. Being Muslims we were subjected to extensive background checks. The arrogance of Israelis and their contempt for the people whose land they occupy was evident.

Whenever I see injustice or corruption I send letters to our local Express newspaper, along my name and address. This worries my family, especially when I expose or criticize the high and mighty. I'm not one to bury my head in the sand and say, "This doesn't concern me." My most recent letter addressed the present genocide in Gaza, where the death toll has crossed 30,000 civilians, mainly women and children. Meanwhile, the world watches and complains, but does nothing. No one wants to offend the Jews.

Israel-Hamas conflict: leaders must support 2-state solution

WE all condemned the slaughter of innocent civilians in southern Israel by Hamas on October 7. However, one must wonder what would drive people to do such a thing.

In 1948 the British, who held a mandate over Palestine, decided to divide the country in two. Half went to the Jews, and the Palestinians were left with the other half. Arabs in the new state of Israel were driven off land they owned for centuries and forced to live in refugee camps, where they remain to this day.

The Palestinians, with the help of their Muslim neighbours, attempted to regain their land in 1967. They failed, with Israel occupying *all* of Palestine. Despite several UN resolutions telling them to leave, they remain there. They continue to build illegal settlements on the occupied territories in order to cement their position.

UN resolutions haven't worked. Peace talks haven't worked. Terror tactics haven't worked. What are the Palestinians supposed to do?

The Israelis have one of the most modern armies in the world. They receive unconditional support from American politicians, who depend on Jewish wealth to get elected. Any attempt to pressure them is met with accusations of "anti-Semitism". They are quick to invoke the Holocaust as an excuse to do whatever they please. It is ironic that a people, who were persecuted for thousands of years, see nothing wrong in oppressing others.

Rabbi Dovid Weiss and other Jewish clerics, point out the difference between Judaism and Zionism. Zionism is a political, non-religious nationalistic movement dedicated to creating a home for Jews. It doesn't matter if it means taking someone else's property. Judaism opposes the creation of a Jewish state. It's about obeying the will of God, which doesn't involve a Jewish homeland.

While America is quick to help Ukraine defend itself against its Russian occupiers, it supports the Zionists who are occupying Palestine. What hypocrisy! Right now they are sending nuclear armed naval vessels to support the Israelis, as if they needed help.

As much as the present carnage is regrettable, I hope it pricks the conscience of world leaders to actively support a two-state solution. If not there will be, as Bob Marley predicted, "war in the east, war in the west".

G Barrow
Valsayn

Epilogue

My last flight, November 2013

Khalid, posing with someone's Black Hawk

Unlike my well-coordinated son Khalid, who grew up playing PS4 video games, I was not a natural pilot. I got into aviation purely by chance. It was my ticket out of Malick. As such, I struggled and progressed slowly. Fortunately, I had some first-class instructors to help me along the way.

The list is long, but I would like to pay special tribute to Captain Roger Grell. I've often found that the most knowledgeable people are also the most humble. This was true of 'Uncle Rog.' The fact that he's called 'Uncle' by black, brown and blue alike shows the high esteem in which he is held. Despite his stature he was down to earth, and we all enjoyed his delightful company. I know of only one other captain who achieved that exalted status. That was Captain Robert Franco, 'Uncle Bob', another training officer of rare integrity.

You may get the impression while reading this narrative that I didn't always think things through. You may be right. My philosophy was, "go through hard and see what happens." If things went south I could either fix it, cover it up or distance myself. Our mantra in those days was, "Deny, deny, deny", despite overwhelming evidence to the contrary. I didn't want to die wishing, "If only I'd done this or that". Instead I want to go with an enigmatic smile on my face thinking, "Boy, you really did that shit?" (See 'Boy Days, Vol 2', to be released after my demise.)

There were a few instances in which I actually made the right move. Most important was marrying Shaheeba. I'm not a soppy person, but I'll quietly admit that my love, admiration and respect for her knows no bounds. I'll never tell her that since I don't want her to get swell-headed and think she's too good for me. While her cooking skills leave much to be desired, she somehow managed to spawn three viable offspring. These have gone on to become highly qualified professionals, of whom I am most proud.

My elder son Mickhaiel, an open scholarship winner, spent half his life in Cambridge and Oxford to become a consultant histopathologist like his Mama. There he met his equally brilliant wife, Tanzilah, a consultant radiologist.

My second son Khalid is married to a lovely girl, Anushka, who is my dentist. I am so relaxed in her chair I sometimes fall asleep.

Daughter Sofiya is a doctor and is currently writing her postgrad exams. She is my personal physician. I don't let anyone else come near me with a needle.

Sprangers, pipers and home invaders may see them, with their nice homes and fancy cars, and gripe, "How come dem have all dat?" The answer is simple – hard work and sacrifice. Try it sometime.

In closing it may seem that this book's title is misleading since it covers my whole life and not just my boy days. That's because I haven't grown up yet.

Acknowledgements

Many thanks to: -

Neil Chin Aleong, *Ex QRC Head Boy and life-long friend, for editing this book.*

Emmanuel Davis, *TTAC executive member and Graphic Artist, for designing the covers.*

Cote' ci Cote', T&T Dictionary, *an invaluable reference for my glossary*

Google and Chat GPT, *for fact checking my historical references.*

Apendix A

Glossary of Trini words and expressions, which I've spelled as pronounced.

AA, Whey!	**expressions of surprise**
A la vive	type of fishing using live bait
Accra	salt-fish fritters
Agouti	large rodent, hunted as wild meat
Ah	I, a, of
Ah dey	I'm here, I'm fine
Ah done	I'm finished
Ah go blaze yer tail	I will beat you
Ah go do fuh yuh	I will get back at you
Ah going to come back	I'll be back soon
Ah never see more	expression of surprise and anger
All ah all yuh, all ah we	everybody
All dat in it	accept the fact
All dis time, all now	meanwhile, at present
All fours	popular card game
All how	every way
Aloes	medicinal plant
Aloo	potato
Alpagat	cheap sandal made of rope
Amchar	spicy masala condiment
An dem	and those others
An ting	and so on
Answer back	being rude to parents
Arepa	trini word for empanada
Asking answers	asking the obvious
Ax meh dat	I agree with you
B from bull foot	**confused, not knowing anything**
Babash	potent bush rum
Back squeezing	giving less than agreed
Bad drive	to drive recklessly
Bad eye, stink eye	evil eye
Bad John	a violent or aggressive individual
Bad mind	holding a grudge
Bad talk, bad mouth	speak ill of someone, gossip
Baigan	eggplant, melongene

Bailna	rolling pin used for making roti
Bacchanal	conflict, confusion
Back back	to reverse a car
Bad skylark	bad practical joke
Bagasse	cane trash
Bake	dough, fried or roasted
Bake an shark	popular dish, at Maracas bay
Balisier	heliconia flower
Ball head	bald
Bamboozle	to confuse and fool someone
Bamsee, bam bam. bum bum,	backside bottom
Ban yuh belly, jaw	prepare for hard times
Bat grog	consume a large quantity of rum
Battle axe	formidable woman
Battymamzel	dragon fly
Batty man, buller	male homosexual
Barra	Soft flour bake used in doubles
Bawl dong de place	Scream, like during child birth
Bazodi	not thinking straight
Batee	Indian word for daughter
Beat back	out does, trumps
Beat book	cram for exams
Beat down	bargain for a lower price
Beating pan	playing in a steel band
BeeWee	British West Indian Airways
Behin de bridge	east Port of Spain, a bad john area
Behin god back	living way out in the country
Belly wokin	gripes, diarrhea
Benne balls	hard Tobago candy
Beraa	gold bracelet worn by granny
Betaa	Indian son
Better belly buss dan good food waste	excuse to eat everything
Better fete	even better than expected
Better you dan me	I prefer if you take the risk
Bhaji	spinach
Big Pappy	important man
Big unks	large marble used as a taw
Big up	promote
Bird pick	fruit which birds have eaten
Bird pepper	small hot peppers
Bite-up	upset, in a foul mood
Black cake	Christmas cake soaked in rum

Blasted or damn vex	extremely angry
Blank	avoid or dismiss someone
Blaze	plenty pepper in your doubles
Bligh	an ease up
Block	area where drugs are sold
Block and tackle	bicycle game to see who could balance
Blood eh take	instant dislike for someone
Blue food	local cuisine
Blue fly	iridescent flies that lay eggs on meat
Blues	X rated movie
Board house	cheap simple house made of wood
Bobol	government corruption
Bobolee	a stuffed effigy of Judas
Body line	curvy shape of a woman
Bois	stick used by stick-fighters
Bois bande	bark used for treating erectile dysfunction
Boldface, brass face	bold, brash, arrogant
Boil dong like bhagi	to simmer down or reduce in size
Bong to	must do
Bongo	drums and associated dance
Boo boo man	character used by parents to frighten kids
Bootoo	a baton carried by a policeman
Borse man	lady person in authority
Bosse back	deformed spine
Bottle and spoon	utensils used to beat out a calypso rhythm
Bouff, bouff up	reprimand
Bounce, butt meh head	made a bad choice
Box bass	bass instrument made with a box
Box cart	wooden trolley using bearings for wheels
Box lunch	pre-packaged meals served in schools
Brakesin	trying to avoid doing something risky
Bramble	to deliberately confuse an issue
Breaking beesh	skipping classes
Brer Anancy	spider character in folk tales
Bring off	quarrel, get on bad
Brokes	having no money
Broko	person walking with a limp
Brudderman, Breds	friend, acquaintance
Brush, Doh rush de brush	casual sex
Brushing cutlass swiper	a blade on a stick for cutting grass
Buff proof	not affected by rejection
Buljol	dish with salt-fish, onions and tomatoes

Bull pistle	leather whip made from the penis of a bull
Bumper	large woman's bottom
Bunout, bun	exhausted after running
Bun bun	the burnt bottom of a pot of pelau
Buse up	to abuse and insult someone
Bush bart	Herbal bath to wash away spirits
Buss a lime	go out with friends
Bussin bamboo	igniting wet carbide
Buss head	bleeding head injury
Bussup shut	paratha roti, served with curry
Bussing yer brains	having to think hard

Calabash	**large nut shell**
Callalou	green slimy dish made with ochro
Candle fly	fire fly
Carete	popular tasty fish
Cascadoo	bony river fish
Cassava pone	dense cassava pudding
Cat in bag	buying something unseen
Cata-boil	an eye swelling
Chaconia	our national flower
Chain head	to fool and influence someone
Chataigne	large legume boiled or curried
Chile fada	father of the baby, often denied
Chillibibi	snack made of ground corn
Chin, Chinee	owner of any Chinese restaurant
Chinksin,	economizing
Chinky, chinksy	tiny
Chip chip	small shells found in Mayaro
Choof choof	inedible puffer fish
Chook fire	making things worse
Chow	spicy snack made with mango
Chupid, chupidee	stupid
Chutney	spicy sauce to put on doubles
Clean forget	forgotten completely
Coal pot	cast iron stove used for roasting
Cockset	coils, lit to repel mosquitoes
Cocksure	positive, very sure
Cocoa tea	hot chocolate drink made cocoa
Cocoa panyol	Venezuelan cocoa estate worker.
Cocoyea	spine of the coconut leaf,
Cocrico	National bird of Tobago

Coki eye	cross eyed
Cold like dog nose	when your coffee or tea gets cold
Cooking with gas	things finally going right
Coolie	name for an east Indian
Coolin	drink that cools the blood
Come go	come with me
Coming to come	coming along well so far
Compere	old friend
Constable	policeman of any rank
Coral snake	colorful poisonous snake
Corbeau	common black vulture
Corbeau doh eat sponge cake	not appreciating something good.
Corbeau pee on yuh	jinxed
Cow heel	cow's hoof used soups and stews
Country bokee come to town	an unsophisticated person
Court clothes	formal wear
Crab back	tasty expensive dish made with crab meat
Cramps your style	inhibits you
Crapaud	large ugly toad
Crapo fish	inedible rock fish too often caught
Crapo foot	bad handwriting
Crapo smoke yer pipe	you are in big trouble
Creole	local African influenced or related
Crick, crack, the wire bend	that's the way the story ends.
Crix	popular biscuit, usually eaten with cheese
Cro Cro	small tasty fish.
Crocus bag	large canvas bag used to make hammocks
Current	getting sexual vibes from someone
Cross thread	misbehaved
Curry chicken, goat, beef, shrimps	put in a wrap roti or in a buss up shot box
Curry tabanka	moping over an Indian girl,
Cut arse, tail	a good licking
Cut eye	look of disapproval or anger
Cutlass, gilpin	machete
Cunumoonu	a simple-minded person from the country
Cyar	can't
Cyar make	can't manage
Cyar see mehself	don't think I'll be able
Da, dat	**that**
Dada	head
Dan dan	fancy clothes, such as your Sunday best

Darkers	shades
Dasheen bush	large leaves used to make callalou
Dat beat all	that beats everything
Dat is man	man with an impressive achievement
De damn ting self	the real thing, just what I needed
Ded out tired,	expired
Deputy outside lover,	considered essential
Dem say, dey say, town say	what people are saying
Dew falling	reason to cover a baby's head
Dey	location, as in "whey ya dey?"
Dey	they, them, their
Deyas	small clay pots, lit with oil during Divali
Dhalpuri	roti with split peas inside
Dahl belly	Indian man with a large paunch
Die like a semp	a horrible death, with your feet in the a
Digging blues	worried, depressed
Digging horrors	having a hard time
Dish up	finish something quickly, like an easy job
Divali	Hindu festival of light
Donkey's years	a long time ago
Do fer ya	threatened revenge
Dog cheap	a bargain
Dog doh make cat	children take after their parents
Doh dig nuttin	don't you worry
Doh talk bout	don't even mention
Doh try dat, doh come wid dat	don't try to fool me
Doh even tink	get that idea out of your head
Donkey's years	a very long time
Doo doo darlin	term of endearment
Doubles	breakfast made with two barra and channa
Dong de place	the surrounding area
Dong de islands	the islands on the north-western peninsula
Dong de road	near by
Dongs	small fruit, best eaten when overripe
Donkey eye	seed which gets hot when you rub it
Dotish, dodo head	stupid, uneducated.
Douen	folklore creature with feet facing back
Dougla	half African, half Indian
Dry so?	just so?
Dry River	large river bordering east Port of Spain
Duck in	make a quick stop or visit
Dulahin	young Indian bride

Duncy head | not too bright in school
Dus it, split de scene, clock out | to leave

Ease up | **a little help**
Eat ah food | unexpected good fortune
Eat parrot bottom | talking excessively
Eclip | eclipse, thought to affect pregnancies
Eh no joke, eh making joke | this is serious
Enless | plenty
Every dog bad in he own yard | easy to be brave when you have backup
Every man jack | everyone
Even self | even if
Extempo | composing calypso verses on the fly
Eye bigger dan yeh belly | taken more food than you could eat
Eye food, eye candy | a pretty woman

Fada | **father**
Fatigue | tiredness, teasing
Farse an outta place | getting involved in things
Feeling ah how | not feeling comfortable
Fete match | sport event with alcohol
Fit like yam | a perfect fit
Fire de wuk | leave the job
Five cents shave ice on a hot pavement | worth very little
Fix up | do what is required
Flambo | light made using a bottle and kerosene
Flim | film
Follow fashion | copy cat
Francomen | frankly speaking
Force ripe | fruit prematurely ripened, precocious
Fresh water yankee | speaking with an American accent
Free up | relax and enjoy yourself
French creoles | off white locals
Fry dry | small fish coated in flour and fried
Full ah mout | talking big with no action
Fur so | plenty, excess
Fus ah glad | I'm so happy

Galavant | **to go roaming all over the place**
Gallery | to show off
Gas brain | a loose woman who likes fancy cars
Gauva season | hard times

Gazette paper	old news print, used as toilet tissue
Geera pork	spicy curry dish
Geeze, gee whiz, geeze	an expression of surprise
Getting on ignorant	acting stupidly, being unreasonable
Gimmee	give me
Give jack his jacket	give someone the credit he deserves
Goat mout	to jinx
Going to come back	returning soon
Good fer yuh	you got what misfortune you deserve
Go thru hard	To do something without thinking
Grining	upset about something
Good for yuhself	feeling important
Gorn off	acting crazy
Gorn trou	no longer functional
Grappe	a bunch or handful
Gun talk	threatening speech
Gundy	crab claw, meatiest part

Had wus tuh	**was supposed to do so**
Half dead	limp, tired, lifeless
Han swinging	not contributing
Happy like a pig in shit	ecstatic
Happy like pappy	very pleased
Hard back man	grown man
Harden	stubborn, hard headed
Han to mout	barely surviving
He who rush de brush get brush in ah rush	take your time with a woman
Hear dis talk	listen to this piece of gossip
Hef dis feel	how heavy this is
Hoggish	domineering and unpleasant
Hol some strain	hang on, have some patience
Hops bread	large bun, usually filled with ham
Horn chile	love child
Horner man	outside man, adulterer
Hot foot	can't keep still,
How yer going?	how are you?

If you name man	**if you think you can do it**
Ignorant	unruly, cannot be reasoned with
In ting	likes to be included
In trut	for true
Is dat self	that's the real thing

Is so he stop	that's just the way he is
Is you to ketch	deal with the consequences
It come like if	it's as though
It have none	there's no more left

Jamette, jezebel, skank, jagabat	**a low class woman**
Jashwah	small fish used as live bait
Jaunders	jaundice
Jellit	ice cream on a stick
Jes so?	without asking?
Jig	to try and split an opponent's top
Jigger	a parasite that gets in your toe
Jitney	old time bus or truck
Jokey	funny
Jipney	jeep
Jook, chook	poke
Jooking	board
Jorts	food
Jumbie	spirit
Jus now	hold on a while
Jus so?	without any reason?

Ketch ah vaps	**to do something suddenly**
Ketch ah glad	to be happy
Ketching meh tail, arse, nennen	having it hard
Klim	any brand of powdered milk.
Knocking dog	plentiful, all over the place
Know full well	know very well
Kripsy	crispy
Kuchela	spicy mango appetizer

La basse	**city dump**
Lagniappe	something extra, bonus
Lambi	conch
Lamblass, blaze	to quarrel or beat
Las chile does kill de mudder	the last step always the hardest
Lapp	large forest rodent
Late fuh school head	hair that's difficult to comb
Leggo	let go, release
Lef meh	leave me alone
Lef dat	don't touch
Let the jackass bray	let them talk, it doesn't bother me

Lick dong	to break down or beat up
Like yerself, she go like sheself	happy, she will be very pleased
Lickrish	greedy
Licks like fire	severe beating
Lime, or to go liming	a group of friends hanging out
Look at meh crosses	expression of wonder or surprise
Lord Kitchener	calypsonian, road march king
Lota	fungal skin infestation
Lower dong de radio, TV	turn down the volume

Macajuel effect — **feeling sleepy after a big meal**

Maco	minding other people's business
Maco traffic	traffic caused by a car accident
Maga	undernourished
Mama's boy, Hindu's first born	spoiled child
Man rat	strong man
Manicou	local name or opossum.
Mannish	child being disobedient
Makin hot	the weather is hot
Mamaguy	to fool someone with sweet talk
Mark buss	when the truth comes out
Mash up de place	have fun, cause destruction
Mauby	drink made from tree bark
Maxi taxi	mini buse
Me eh know	don't ask me
Me too	cheap old fashioned cell phone
Megrane	bad headache
Meh dogs dead	I'm in big trouble
Menses	menstruation
Miserable	difficult person
Monkey know which tree to climb	*More* know which side to take
better	even better
Morish tasty food,	makes you want more
Morocoy	local name for a tortoise
Movay lang	To bad talk
Much up	flatter
Mudder	prefix to most trini cuss words

Nah boy — **end to a sentence**

Nah man	no
Nail jook	stepping on a rusty nail
Nancy story	a fake excuse

Nara	stomach pain
Neemakharam	an ungrateful person
Never see, come see	person imitating everything
Never see more	dumfounded
New bran	brand new
Nose hole	nostril
Not easy	capable, very smart
Not for hell	no way
Not me an you	keep far from me
Not one ass	not one thing
Now fur now, now self	right away

Obzokie	**ugly, out of shape**
Oh gyad	when smelling something nasty
Oh lorse, shit, shucks	expression of dismay
Oil dong	savory dish made with breadfruit,
Ole talk	casual talk which may not be true
Ol' time kaiso	vintage calypsos
Ol' mas	everything has gone wrong
One han doh clap	it takes two to do something
One pot	an all in one meal
One time	right away
Ooman	woman
Oui	placed at the end of a sentence
Out ah timing	getting on badly
Out ah place	rude, not knowing your place
Oval	Venue for test matches

Pacro water, tea	**soup made from a mollusk, aphrodisiac**
Papesy bland,	unimpressive
Pappy show	farce, confusion
Pardner	good friend
Parlour	mini-mart
Parlour juice	watered down orange juice
Pass fuh meh	pick me up along the way
Pastelles	dish made with corn flour and meat
Peckish	feeling for something to nibble on
Pelau	national dish made with rice and chicken
Petit careme	short dry season in September
Picong, fatigue	light hearted teasing
Picoplat, semp	song birds kept as pets in wooden cages
Piece ah meh	mind severe reprimand

Pigeon toe, spanner toe	walking with toes pointing inwards.
Pika	thorn in your hand or foot
Piper	drug addict who steals to support his habit
Pirogue	traditional boat design
Pissin tail	small and out of place
Pitch oil	kerosene
Plannase	to hit with the flat side of a cutlass
Play whey	lottery with bets based on dreams
Please God	with God's help
Poc a poc	bit by bit
Polouri	fried balls made with flour and split peas
Pomcetay	fruit with spiky seed
Pone	pudding made with cassava and coconut
Popo	the spoon you use to stir your pot.
Pot spoon	name for a toddler
Pothong, dustbin terrier	common breed dog, easy to maintain
Potty mout, stink mout	uses foul language
Press	shaved ice dipped in red and yellow syrup
Prestige school	a top school, usually denominational
Project, CEPEP, URP	temporary ten days' employment
Provision, ground provision	yam, dasheen, sweet potato, eddoe
Puddin	spicy dish made with pig's blood
Puja	Hindu prayer ceremony
Pull ah vein	common ailment, caused by straining
Pullin bull, running PH	operating an unauthorized taxi
Punchin	white rum with high alcohol content
Pushing a move, trying a ting	checking out a girl
Put ah han	help me out
Put him so	that's just the way he is
Pumpkin vine family	extended family, who may not be related
Puttigal	portugal fruit

Quenk	**wild boar, dangerous to hunt**

Rag up	**to make fun of**
Rakatang	old, broken down
Rain fly	flying ants seen after heavy rain
Rain setup	looks like it might rain
Raise meh blood	get me vex
Ramfle	to make untidy
Ramsack	ransack
Rat cheese	cheddar

Razor grass	tall grass with sharp leaves
Red man, woman	mixed race people in high demand
Red mango	preserved mango, dyed red,
Reverse back	to reverse your car
River lime	outing with friends by a river
Road march	tune played most often during carnival
Roas bake	coconut bake, roasted, not fried
Roll on roll off	fully assembled foreign used cars
Roti	dhalpuri or paratha bake
Rubbers	condoms
Rudeness	sexual activity
Rum punch	cocktail made with rum, lime and syrup
Run somting nah man	give me some
Running taxi	making a living as a taxi driver
Run yuh mout	bad talk, spill the beans

Sada roti	**bake, filled with vegetables.**
Saga boy	young man all dressed up
Saheena	dish made with flour and dasheen bush
Salt prune	spicy Chinese prunes preserved in salt
Same khaki pants	same situation
San fly	tiny fly that bites
Santapee	centipede,
Sappy	soft and runny
Savannah	large open ground in the heart of POS
Schooch,	game where you hit others with a ball
Say wha	whatever
Scorpion pepper	hot pepper used to make pepper spray
Scrunter	someone barely getting by
Seow	soy sauce
Set ah	large set of
Shado beni, bandania	seasoning herb used in every trini dish.
Shave ice	ground ice used to make sno cones
Shining bush	herb used as a cure for everything
Shit talk	talking nonsense with friends
Short drop	short taxi ride
Shitup	to insult someone, to screw up a job
Shitong, shit snake	foolish person of no importance
Sick	not easy to deal with
Skull	con
Slack	lazy, unproductive
Slackness	corruption

Slight	little pepper in your doubles
Smallie	school girl, easy target
Smart man	con man
Smell ah rat	to be suspicious
Snake in de grass	someone not to be trusted
Soca	loud party music with meaningless lyrics
Sof drink	flavored soda
Sometimish	fickle, being unfriendly sometimes
Sorrell	sweet red Christmas drink
So so	not too bad
Sou Sou	a community banking arrangement
Soubriquet	name calypsonians give to themslves
Souse	spicy dish made by boiling pig's parts
Sparrow	greatest calypsonian in the world
Sou sou	community saving scheme
Stale drunk	hung over
Stale joke	one you've heard many times before
Stan pipe	a roadside tap for the community
Stan up on meh chess	food that's hard to digest
Steups, chups	rude dismissive sound
Storm	gate crash
Straight case	without a doubt
String ban	having a lot of children
Strimps roti	a wrapped roti with curried shrimps
Spanish	person of mixed undetermined race
Spinnin top in mud	doing something that won't work
Sponge off	being bathed with a sponge
Spranger	petty thief
Solo	popular soft drink.
Soucouyant	a folklore blood sucking old woman
Spirit lash	delayed consequences of your actions
Star boy	the hero in a movie
Step on someone's corns	to do something to create enmity
Suckeye	dead simple
Sweat rice	food using a woman's bodily fluids
Sweet bread	tasty bread made with fruit preserves
Sweet eye	blink to attract someone's attention
Tabanka	being heartbroken, may cause suicide
Take advantage,	to bully or cheat
Take infront before infront take you	to act before something happens to you
Tanty	aunt or any old person

Tattoo	local name for armadillo
Taw	your favorite marble
Tawa	thick aluminum or iron griddle
Theatre	cinema
Tief head	to fool someone
Tiger cat	ocelot. Few, if any, left in the wild.
Toe jam	what you get from unwashed feet
Too too	excrement
Totee	sexual organ
Toting	having the blues over a lost love
Town say	the latest that people are saying
Trini to the bone	a native of T&T engrossed in our culture
Tru tru	real, genuine
Try ah ting	give it a shot, usually with a woman
Try all how	tried my best
Tun tun	a vagina, also a stupid person
Tun ole mas	everything gone wrong
Twenty four hours	garden lizard
Two by four	pitch pine lumber measuring 2 x 4 inches
Two shits	what you couldn't care less about
Two twos	in no time

Uncle	**a term of respect for any older person**
Under heavy manners	under close supervision
Use up, waste dong	to waste something
Ups an go	leave suddenly
Upteen	many
Unks	big marble

Vamping	**smelling bad**
Vaps	all of a sudden
Village ram	man who has sex with many women
Veni	Venezuelan immigrant
Vex money	backup cash in case on a date

Wajang, jaggerbat, scank	**low class woman**
We doh live so	you don't have to thank or pay me
We go pick up	I'll see you again
Well I never	expression of surprise
Well yes	expression of amazement
Who tell me say that?	I shouldn't have said that
Wetman	womanizer. Tiida car

Wahbeen	river fish, wanton woman
Wajang	low class person
Watch meh good	take good note
Wha happenin dey?	what's going on?
What doh kill does fatten	safe to eat
What scene you on?	why are you like that?
What in the road is dog own	finders keepers
What monkey see monkey do	being a follow fashion
When yuh miss meh ah gorn	I'll be leaving soon
Whey?	what?
where?	why?
Which part?	where did you put something?
Whiteman	un-bleeding scrape
Wining	sexually explicit dancing at fetes
What monkey see monkey do	being a follow fashion
What jail is this?	what nonsense am I hearing?
Who is you? Who you feel you is?	who do you think you are?
Who say dem say	stupid useless argument
Wotless	crazy and irresponsible

Yam — ground provision

Yampee	crusted mucus in the eye
Yard fowl	free roaming chicken
You self	you should know better
Yuh askin answers	you're asking the obvious
Yuh arse dark, yuh dogs dead	you are in big trouble
Yuh business fix	everything is sorted out
Yuh cyar get mango from a calabash tree	you get what you deserve
Yuh eh easy nuh	you are capable of anything
Yuh fadder is a glass maker?	you're blocking my view
Yuh go fine out	threaten to do something later
Yuh look fer dat	you got what you deserved
Yuh mad in yuh arse	are you crazy?
Yuh makin joke	you can't be serious
Yuh see me? I dun	count me out
Yuh tink it easy?	it's harder than you think

Zaboca — avocado

Zandolie, twenty fours hours	garden lizard.
Zangie	fresh water eel
Zwill	Home made spinner

About the author

Gerry Barrow lives in Tinidad with his wife, Shaheeba, and three children, Mickhaiel, Khalid and Sofiya. He taught science and machine shop at Malick Composite school for one year, after which he won a government scholarship to train as a pilot.

Immediately on graduation from flying school he was hired with the national Airline, BWIA, now called Caribbean Airlines. He flew many different types of aircraft, from turbo-props to jets, and retired after 32 years.

Gerry has a wide range of interests, no doubt inspired by his father, Dr. Russell Barrow, who was an expert on everything. In introducing Gerry to a group of scientists, an astronomer friend said, "If I told you all Gerry does we'll be here whole day."

'Boy Days' covers his life in Glencoe, starting at age five, through primary school, college, university in Jamaica, flying school and hair raising experiences in the air and at sea. All stories are true.

At age 70 he is still going strong, getting involved in new things all the time. Right now he's doing a course in cytology and learning to play the Flugel horn.